THE COMPLETE COLLECTION
OF A ROBOT (1)

SEARCHING FOR NIRMANA
WITH SMART FINGERS

SHARIF AL-SHAFIEY

ISBN 978-1-936373-59-8
Published in the United States by Unbound Content, LLC,
Englewood, NJ.
Cover design: ©2017 Mohamed Ammar
Author photo: ©2017 Mifrani Abdelhaq
Translated by Amr El-Zawawy
The work in this collection is original and was previously published
in Arabic.

SEARCHING FOR NIRMANA WITH SMART FINGERS
First edition 2017

UNBOUND
CONTENT

Publisher's Note

The decision to present this book in a somewhat nontraditional format was made to preserve the look of the author's original work and to provide a visual cue for its theme: the relationship between the real and virtual worlds. This book is an exploration of humanity and man's attempts to improve upon it (perfect it?) through the use of technology. At its core though, it seeks to lay bare that which transcends man's clumsy manipulations: the heart. Please enjoy these meditations on man and machine.

—Annmarie Lockhart

TABLE OF CONTENTS

"Searching With Highly Modernist Poetry for an Extinct Dream"
(Article by Lebanese Critic Dr George Juha, Reuters)

The Egyptian poet Sharif Al-Shafiey's latest collection may be considered a unique one in the Arabic language. While times are lost, and the poems are on the verge of extinction, the poetic language used appears to be a mixture of the time of 'mechanical' dreams and the extinct time itself.

It is a poetic collection that carries within point- and- counterpoint. The poet uses the jargon and terminology of the Internet, and thus searches for a world driven to semi-oblivion by another strong world which appears to be widely and deeply dominant over the imagination of the people of the 'universal village' and even over their language.

Before speaking about the content of the present collection, we can shed light on its cover and title. The cover is a very expressive artwork which summarizes much of what the poems are about. Up to the right of the poet's name are a few words on a poetic collection yet to come: "The Complete Collection of a Robot (1)"; then there is the word 'poetry'. Then comes the title "Searching for Nirmana with Smart Fingers". A subtitle, more succinct, reads: "200 Web Attempts to Hunt Down an Extinct Being". The word 'web' might be daunting to those who fancy as a fearful expression or a psychological state. Yet it is part of the Internet jargon.

Much of the cover, which is designed by Patric Tarabeya, is a human-cum-artificial hand. Its veins and arteries are made up of several metal wires, and its black fingers hold with the thumb, index finger and middle finger a colorful, radiant ball, i.e. the globe. To the bottom corner of the cover is an image taken from the Yahoo search page, where the hit reads: "Search results: Nothing Found for Nirmana".

Inside the book, we find that we are still in the world of the Internet. Each poem carries a title starting with the word "search", followed by a cardinal number. What is more, the print style and the font are computer-like.

It is worth mentioning here that Arab poets, since the mid sixties, especially the Lebanese Adel Khoury, have been trying to indite what they called 'The Electronic Poem' in an attempt to emulate the outer space atmosphere and the obsession with physics.

Before asking what the name 'Nirmana' means, and before being driven away to believing that is denotative of 'Nirvana' or the world of transcendentalism or the extinct dream, we must first notice that the poet has used the two names and more to mean one thing: a new impossibility added to the Ghoul, the Phoenix and so forth(1).

In his poetry, Al-Shafiey is sometimes bitterly sarcastic and other times ironic. But between the two, we find a fine line of pain, despair and searching for a lost time amidst what seems to be alien or even connotative of meaninglessness.

In "Search 2", we read:
I asked her:
"Who are you?"

She said:
"I am myself."

She asked me:
"Who are you?"

I said:
"I am you."

Waves overwhelmed Nirmana; she yelled at me:
"Keep to your flat;
Turn off the water clasp quickly!"

In "Search 3", and before changing the names, we read:

Just like you are summoned easily in my conscience
(Which is not grammatically justifiable),
On the back of a pacified elephant,
So you seep easily into the pores of my cracked skin.
My interconnected atoms soak you up,

---

[1] In the Arabic tradition, there are three impossibilities: the Ghoul, the Phoenix, and the faithful companion.

8

My atoms which are eager to be soluble
Into quicklime.

After the introduction where the scientific and the 'linguistic' are crammed like barriers in the face of love and dreams, we reach the diverse names of "Nirmana", written in Arabic then in Latin characters, like what is being searched for on the Internet.

The poet writes, being deep on the Web:

You comb your hair irritably before me,
While I quietly press the keys of the computer keyboard.
I write the letters of your name in the search engine "Yahoo":
Nirmana
Nirma
Nirmitta
Nitta
Mitta
Titta
Nirmala
Nirvana
Nirva
Noreena
Noritta
Narmitta
Narmina
Nermina
Noon
Nona
N

The screen answers back with a smile
Like ships' projectiles
With two wings and a tail,
Yet unable to fly.

What does Al-Shafiey mean here? Does he mean that there is no space for dreams with all their names and types? Does he mean the reverse, but we are unaware? This vagueness may be the very answer. Yet in "Search 5", for example, the answer becomes more illustrative, or this what seems to be for the reader. We are in a world much like 'implanting dreams' artificially.

He writes:
I am in no need to conquer the space
For I already possess over a thousand satellite channels
In my bedroom.
(Perhaps these satellite channels are those
Who possess and imprison my humanness
With all its successive phases).

I am still in need of conquering Nona
And plunging into its tissues in a spacesuit,
After the dish and the decoder have failed
In dealing with its nearby, strong signals!

But perhaps after death there is a certain 'resurrection'. In 'Search 181', the lines read:

When the truth is stupid,
Man clutches to stupidity
Not to believe it.

So,
When the Nirmana's pieces were distributed
To all nations of the world,
I clutched to the myth of Isis and Osiris.
I am still waiting the day
I collect the scattered parts of my charming one,
And mount her body anew.

Does Al-Shafiey mean all what we have thought we have understood some of it, or is meaning still away from all that? The reader has fallen prey to searching for Nirmana in other poems.

"A Poem Under the Echo of Surprises"
(Article by Lebanese Writer and Poet Shawqi Abi Shaqra)

The poet in question is Sharif Al-Shafiey, the author of the collection Searching for Nirmana with Smart Fingers. His poetry is new in that the poet is characterized by a uniqueness of narratology and of preserving humor as well as going forward to the fountain of poetry without leaving a void in the process of word-smithing and in the witticisms strewn hither and thither.

He does not silence himself, but speaks humorously with an acute sense of consciousness. He does not relent in his narration throughout the collection, nor does he doff the garb of earnestness in the midst of pristine lyricism, which is taken from the poeticism that grants us a true image of what boils up inside the Arab young psyche, the psyche that is immersed in lovelorn poetry, in speaking up.

Yet the poet does not pretend to be so; rather he expands his tale, his speech, and his poem. He observes none but himself, for through this he appears to be all the more different. He does not take any rest in his quest, but links things, meanings and hidden drawings all together. By delving more into this, we feel much more involved in observing him, in turning around, in drowning and in walking along, stricken by eagerness and quietude. We are thus ready to pick up the rare sparrow or the little bird that informs us and brings glad tidings, where the collection is full of such tidings.

Al-Shafiey is after that wont: creating ambivalence between easiness and difficulty, prowess and meaty experience, as if taking hold of a fact, willy-nilly, or yelling sulkily. The poet never sticks to the space around him, but excels over himself, goes faster than possibilities and meanderings, approaching the public cause, extending his head from individualism to the world of collectiveness and spontaneity. He sharpens his pen and his talent to be verily individualistic. He always seeks the 'spring of writing', a poetical existence based on familiar phraseology, and on trying to be creative when it is too difficult or too demanding to do so.

All his poetic architecture is full of veracity, and his spontaneity is contiguous to another one. He only grieves for himself, for the different content which stems from the self and collides with reality, with the latent perplexity in the abstract and in all and sundry.

Al-Shafiey is as yet young: his pen is drizzling and pouring wishes and other characteristics. He is saddened by nothing; he may let those who depart do so from all around him; he leaves the poem under the echo of surprises, with the intention of creating new things to be unfamiliar and away from faintness, or even struggle, until reaching the destination.

I am pleased with the poet, for he has gleaned something from some distance, and for he has realized, as a forerunner for his coevals and predecessors, who he is. He also realizes what the game is; he has in his present collection gestures and small strikes wider than that; he has textual moments that are sonorous and highly uniform. Doubtless, the poet has a special certainty, a special diction that does not collide with the barriers or slide down technical pitfalls. In this aspect, he may be starting from and ending at a certain originality.

He has the right to set a trend and call his colleagues and readers to share. We are here prone to praise the poet's style and to be amongst those who rise up wide-awake and adopt a stilted writing style that is similar to the raspberry bush where fruits glisten and where colors are galore. Everyone is intent on gleaning a color, a palatable fruit, a scrumptious meal.

"Al-Shafiey: A Peaceful Putsch in the Arabic Poetry"
(Article by Algerian Writer and Critic Salim Boufendassa)

In his Searching for Nirmana with Smart Fingers: 200 Web Attempts to Hunt Down an Extinct Being "The Complete Collection of a Robot (1)", the Egyptian poet Sharif Al-Shafiey provides a unique poetic experience in Arabic poetry.

Al-Shafiey did not only provide such a fine contribution, but has also opened up unpopulated vistas for poetry, and has placed us in a climate difficult to escape, since Nirmana, the virtual child of light, has become a curse that befalls all those who have read the sacred book of our fellow robot.

It is the fourth contribution by this poet, who has astounded the Egyptian poetic circles with three collections: Between the Two of Them, Time Gets Rusty, All by Himself, He Listens to the Concert of Chemistry, and Colors Tremble Covetously. He is ready to release Laughing Gases, the second part of The Complete Collection of a Robot.

The poetical biography of the light-hearted robot opens with a strange dedication: 'To the musty air which forced me to open the window'. And surely the windows will be opened, and we will give in to the successive epical light-whiffs. We are never bored, since it simply ceases not to astonish us one line after the other:

I have been driving my car for ten years
So skillfully that roads have envied me!

The surprise which hugged me tight
Is that I have failed the driving test abroad!

The cop told me that
I had gazed at the mirror.
I answered that I was in fact not to blame:
Nirmana was sitting on the back seat!

Though I didn't get the license,
I felt indescribably happy,
For I have been trained to drive myself
On exceptional errands.

There is always a woman on the backseat, trying to manage the game, but here she is completely different like the ever-changing Nirmana. And definitely their joint 'life project' will be different and interesting:

Behind Nirmala who is extending before me like a screen
I clearly see life and death on the stage
Swapping seats and roles,
And myself approaching myself in quickened paces.

Is Nirmala that transparent,
Or is she nonexistent?
Nirmana changes her name the way she changes her customs: she is Nirmana, Nirmala, Nirvana, Nirmazad, etc., in order to contain women of all regions, and to contain all symbols and states of love pangs, and to send stunning signals to the lover all the time.

She is the luscious life, the necessary alternative to a monotonous unbearable life, the alternative that the poet invents in a project based on tricky simplicity which discloses the recesses and collects beings and objects in one scene, the Doomsday, when the poet settles his scores with life through a black comedy that recalls the facts in a satirical insinuation. He has given the task to a robot, which has in turn taken the customs of man without being completely human or even a metamorphosed human in the shape of a machine, without giving up his bad habits. But we sympathize with the robotic narrator, and impersonate his habits which are transmitted to us through magnetic signals:

Those dwelling in skyscrapers
Are much taller than me
(According to the pictures taken by imbecilic satellites).
Despite this,
I do not envy them,
Nor are their abodes secure against earthquakes and winds.
I see them in their real shape.
They only see my virtual lineaments,
Which do not serve their interests
In the other side of the globe.

I am dedicated
To reading my palm and tree leaves.
They do not have time for such readings,
And their palms are not engraved,
And their tree leaves are not green.

My lifelong dream is one pearl conch
And to remain in my delicious coma
Away from mortals' noise and blunders.
They are dead beats
Because they want to collect all world's pearls
Legally and illegally.

I love Nirvana,
And indeed believe in her existence.
They like no one to love no one,
And more important for them
Than denying Nirvana's existence
Is denying anyone who does not deny her existence!

The robot attacks life to turn it into poetry whose subject-matter is
dreary life, without embellishment or complexity. Surprisingly
enough, poeticism is achieved through facts and scenes, not
language. Here lies the ingenuity and uniqueness of Al-Shafiey. He
transforms all that encounters him into poetry, depending on a
simple language, which is yet technical and scientific. He strangely
effortlessly invests on that language in such a way that is
unavailable to our age's poets. Perhaps those poets depend on
readymade rhetoric more than on life's subjects: Al-Shafiey does
not depend on books in his laboratory, but on life, which he turns
into a mind-boggling symphony by dint of his chemistry.

In this context, the poet never spares to use commendable means,
which he has applied in the rest of his past contributions (for they
are not whims anymore). Fantasy becomes a familiar image: for
example, he invites us to attend a concert for Alzheimer's patients,
which ends in eating their fingers on delicious dishes. Or he
presents us with a scene where cute killers dissolve children into an
acid solution before excusing themselves politely.

It is important to assure that Al-Shafiey's exotica are not alien. They are logical, being similar to Garcia Marquez's. It is an attempt at ridiculing another imposed life whose strangeness is difficult to accept.

Poetry thus provides an opportunity to deconstruct the world without giving away its tropes or its natural function. Here lies the importance of the poet, which has attracted to him both friends and foes:

In a bee's confessions in the Police Station,
It was reported she is mixing her honey with glucose.

In the flower's confessions in the same station,
It was reported she is mixing her nectar with water.

In my own confessions
At home and under no pressure,
It was reported I am fooling all people,
As I hug them with two arms,
While my true arms are chasing Nona
In the hope of hugging her.

The game ends with the robot's failure to achieve its goal; it does not need consolation, for it is the person indifferent to losses, and it has bet on the multi-named thing to deceive all losses:

Nirmana asked me about my head capital.
I said to her: "You are my head capital."

I asked her about her head capital.
She said: "My capital has no head."

As a final note, words seem to fail in approaching such a rich poetic experience. We will wait for the poet's laughing gases, for he trains us to await him and his poetry. How many poets are there nowadays, but how less poetry is!

"Sharif Al-Shafiey in a Different Language"
(Article by Lebanese Poet and Writer Sabah Zwein)

In the midst of the poetry collections that are released every now and then and are very similar to each other, I happily came across the Egyptian poet Sharif Al-Shafiey's. He is among the few poets whose poetry can be enjoyed for being different. Recently, I have got a copy of the new collection Searching for Nirmana with Smart Fingers. Hardly a page is turned without being lambently surprised at what Al-Shafiey has skillfully and carefully managed. He adopts a new ironic tone as if trying to be familiar with what is unfamiliar to humans. He presents us with a bunch of machines and alien names in order to compose a poem close to the atmosphere which we have become unable to surpass, that is, the computer and all digital gadgetry. Yet Al-Shafiey does not target that machinery, but rather existence in its profound meaning.

Al-Shafiey is a poet of his own way! He has adopted a diction and style out of his own mood, liberty and independence. At first, the reader may think that he is writing about something general and light, but soon we discover from the very first line that he has created an unfamiliar text. He has steered away from hackneyed clichés, yet he does not slide down to the trivialities we daily encounter in poetic and non-poetic books. He does not accept to be similar to his young coevals who thoughtlessly write irresponsibly. He never adopts platitudes and ridiculous expressions like others. He knows that poetry starts at consciousness and difference.

He knows full well that if poetic composition exceeds earnestness, it becomes petty. What he has done, therefore, is freakish, which is not devoid of poetry nonetheless. He has broken away from the usual and the ordinary through machines and robots and all modern technologies only to challenge and be rebellious to everything around. He does not refer to the pendulum, the vacuum cleaner, or Pope Noel, nor does he draw crossword puzzles or write names of girls he has invented from astronomy, astrology and Google, such as Nona, Nirmamana, Nirmitta, Mitta, and Titta only for entertainment —nay, but to face the riskiest of human experiences through the most ironic of the poetic diction.

It is irony through bitterness, but he intends it to be humorous and hostile. The poet paves inaccessible roads, for he sees that the past is unable to encompass modern man's existence through hackneyed expressions. Al-Shafiey wants to have a different expression suitable for the modern young people. He wants a rich, fertile, renewable language, a language through which he can mock the world and all past poetic beliefs. However, his language, though intentionally robot-like and dealing with the world of ugly machines and iron, remains in all its aspects humanly committed and profound enough to be markedly different from obnoxious delirium.

"Al-Shafiey Searches for Nirmana and Composes Poetry for the Digital World With Smart Fingers"
(Article by Saudi Poet and Critic Mohamad Kheder)

In his collection Searching for Nirmana with Smart Fingers "The Complete Collection of a Robot (1)", the poet Sharif Al-Shafiey takes us to new spaces which he employs to make poetry co-extensive with our current affairs, the world of technology and a vastness derived from the modernism of using the digital around us.

Al-Shafiey prefers to read a robot's biography in all its emotional jabs to be the mask through which he presents his poetic images. He moves forward to the source from which he can hunt marginalia and the experiences that pass unnoticed. However, he imbues these spaces and climes with a new guise. Through the slinking steps of Nirvana, her mirrors and his close examination of her states, he carries over his view about life, existence, love and other issues to today's man in a kaleidoscopic, complex world.

The poetic collection at issue can be read as made up of separate poems despite being harmonic and serial. It can be a sort of continual reading according to each theme and intersection between Nirvana and her sensations. Although none of the collection's texts is devoid of the shared theme of Nirvana, who suggests, chooses, argues, thinks and enters into debates with the poetic self in the form of sheer emotionalism, Al-Shafiey says:

Surely, my soul will remain intact
Until Nirvana blows a natural one from her spirit into it,
Then it will be just my size.

It is the poet's desire to shape his text into a new space, into a new visualization harmonic with the smart fingers that search with the robot which carries out the investigations and occupies part of the textual space; it moves and converges with it, convinces us of its mechanisms and extensions, or even composes poetry from all the spaces available for the extensions of visual language in what is technological and automatic. In addition, its language is simple in order to converse with the axiomatic but in a surprising and unexpected ways to be peculiar to the poet or Nirvana. This is clear throughout the collection, for Al-Shafiey says:

Difficultly enough,
I was able to paint a picture
Similar to Nirmana's features
The moment I saw her on the earth.

Ten years later,
The features will certainly be
By 10 years.

Al-Shafiey has opened up a smart space for the poem with smart
fingers in his virtual world. It is a space he invents to find more
poetic spaces vast enough to encompass everything available for the
poetic state. He says:

I am not allowed to eat legumes (all)
So as not to be defeated by fava anemia
And anemia.

I am not allowed Nona (alone)
So as not to be killed by love anemia
Haemorrhage.

This image which is always coupled with Nirvana, Nona or
Nirmana represents at once a state of love and a gateway to life with
all its thoughts and man's surprise at what is ordinary and
extraordinary. Al-Shafiey has differently stopped at this
achievement to imitate, discover and reduce into an emotional
situation. He reminds us of the footage which imagines life
thousands of years from now. It is a reading of the text that
anticipates or speculates. This is clear in the parts in which Nirvana
is suitable for all states and co-extensive with time. We can find the
minute electronic and computerized details of Nirvana through
reading this complete biography where Al-Shafiey traces and
narrates its continuity through a robot or a machine, when it might
become a mathematical equation:

Traditional mathematics
Needs to be reconsidered
After the emergence of special laws of Nirma
To estimate the relative and absolute values.

Or it might become amongst a computer program, a CAT scan or other chemical equations.

The 200 web attempts to hunt an extinct being have been set in 230 pages with a cover that reflects the machine-like nature of the text. The robot's hand holds the globe with its smart fingers to make the entire world within it, to bring us closer to the worlds of this poetic collection and its spaces, and to reveal to us the actual status of today's man in his digital, quickened, fragile, fake life. Spontaneously enough, Al-Shafiey turns his poem into one similar to us, one which poses questions to us to ruminate alongside life and to approach the extinct being the poet examines in all its episodes in search for it.

This complete collection will have a second part entitled Laughing Gases as a new experience co-extensive with his project of searching for the extinct being.

"Al-Shafiey Shakes the Poetic Scene"
(Article by Syrian Poet and Critic Lina Shadoud)

Amidst all our dreams, we have always had the dream of a poem combining between What is realistic and what is virtual, an argumentative poem that answers for the needs of the possible and the impossible, a poem that flirts with imagination, one that flies free away from the restrictions of the form, and takes pleasure in such an escape. There has always been the dream of a poem with self-made laws, with no desire for a particular end; one that does not care about being judged by the others; a poem whose spicy roots are the stem of an inner puzzle. It is thus a poem that swims with wings into invisible universes, which however, exist through texts that breaks all the limits of imagination, producing images that occupy the mind for times to come.

Had it not been for the musty and polluted air, the Egyptian poet Sharif Al-Shafiey would not have opened his window allowing the Nirman virus in, infecting his poems and the lobe of his brain creating strange poetry. Such a virus is apparent in his new poetic collection "SEARCHING FOR NIRMANA WITH SMART FINGERS", the first volume in the poetic work "The Complete Collection of a Robot", where the whole text is narrated by a robot searching for his lost humanity in our suffocating digital world. It was from here that we set off in our journey with him and Nirmana, away from swollen shyness and enslaved humanity through near and strong sings and signals that took control of his nerves and empowered all his defense systems. It was Nirmana who blessed him with an extra tongue in preparation for continuous lighting and diming poems throughout which he used a lot of terms and words that confused us such as "chemically neutral salts", "corruption cases of money laundering", "erosion", "racial discrimination", "genocide" and others. However, such terms are then quickly absorbed by the skills of Al-Shafiey who is infected with the Nirmana Syndrome, lessening the heaviness of the words.

The Nirmana poems have converted his habits and energized him with spiritual Catalysts, with apparent representations in a lively poem with sweat and lachrymal glands, which however reject all attempts for being tamed. It is a free poem, or as he calls it, his illegitimate daughter, or the greatest of his thoughts. We could thus argue that Nirmana is a free poem bounded by no laws, as abiding by laws, in her world, is personified betrayal.

"Nirmana is indeed the most truthful lie!" based on the saying that the sweetest of poetry is that with best lies.

The Nirmana poem has rendered him a victim of "fission reactions", but it has also bisected our understanding and notions about poetry when we sensed his deep and floating desires to compose a poem that has been crawling beneath his skin with a new alphabet making out of him the fantasy champion of a shining poem.

"What you are hearing now is not my voice, nor my muteness. It is the clicking of my iron being with your electrical energy drawn from lightning". It was from there that the flame of "Searching for Nirmana with Smart Fingers" evolved. It is this Nirmana whose love for her, Al-Shafiey does not deny or conceal.
"My lifelong dream is one pearl conch
And to remain in my delicious coma
Away from mortals' noise and blunders.
They are dead beats
Because they want to collect all world's pearls
Legally and illegally.
I love Nirvana".

Nirvana, his own baby child, who has had her first formations in Al-Shafiey's previous poetic works including "Between the Two of Them, Time Gets Rusty" (1994), "All by Himself, He Listens to the Concert of Chemistry" (1996), "Colors Tremble Covetously" (1999) and "The Complete Collection of A Robot" (two books, 2008-2012) with an inspiring mood that is sustained throughout the poetic volume. However, deep in our dreams, we would accept nothing but seeing it as our own dream and vision; what is more is that in many stanzas we do wish that such a kind of work had been ours.

There are some poems that inflame us with the desire to revolt against our own selves, and so does Al-Shafiey's who by no means tries to conceal his desire to revolt against himself and be bilaterally divided as does the amoeba, attempting to revolve around Nirmana "his poem", but how is he to do so when the overall area of Nirmana' map is way larger than the size of his skin as he says?

The poem as written by Al-Shafiey indicates and enhances the existence of charming and magnetic universes that crash in us the tendency for pacifist words. On the contrary, it beseeches us to contemplate the far horizons, and flourishes us with a state of light drunkenness.

"Behind Nirmala who is extending before me like a screen
I clearly see life and death on the stage
Swapping seats and roles,
And myself approaching myself in quickened paces"

The robot insists on proving the existence of Nirmana "The poem", while in a state of self-Schizophrenia, at the time when his real arms are extended to chase her.

It is the Nirmana that has spied on his conscience for the sake of his lost twin:

"Nirmana spied on my conscience
For the sake of my twin lost in jungles
Seven thousand years ago."

Nirmana is the real eraser that eliminates his time table or even the poetry he has always known, his past with all its fears and doubts. He got involved in a state of attack and flee until she has finally haunted him and dissolved in his existence with her own laws that cannot be anatomically read.

He manages to satisfy us by saying that he would not want to build her a statue for fear of having her worshiped and then destroyed; he would instead prefer to swallow her in whole.

In many parts of the poem, the poet manages to break all the boundaries between him and the reader getting very close and more truthful.

"The delicious hot lunch
Which she fed me with her hands in my mouth
(I swear to God, "with her hands in my mouth"!)
He even shares his childhood memories with the reader, since they both are being chased by the Ninja men, the robots and the other mighty powers.

However, once Nirmana has implanted all her laws into his head, she has made her withdrawal. He tried to regain her through the aid of the sieve of his memories with large holes, but all his attempts were in vain, and as a result, coldness occupied his soul. She is gone, and has left her sands and atomic dust on his skin deepening his feelings of nostalgia for her.

"My clean renewable energy
And my nuclear energy
Are allotted to heat my polar soul
To be able to continue to live
After the provisional disappearance of Nirmana
Or depletion forever."

The robot will never recover or be healed as he in reality is her and she in turn is him, and we believe them both.
But what does the cruel hand on the elegant book cover holding the globe by its fingers stand for? Could it be an attempt to crash or throw the globe away? It is the Earth that has become very tight for us that we almost wished we had other planets to live on? Ones that have the alikes of Nirmana on their surfaces?
"Narimana walked barefoot on the mud,
So it was the resurrection of human beings
And hers
While I remained alone in between,
Neither from human beings
Or from Narimana's species."

In of the interviews, Al-Shafiey says, "Greetings to the poem that holds to its identity as a poem; one that acquires its value from its alphabet, not through its ability to flatter with authorities, even if it is the authority of the people ".

Thus, he wants it to be totally pure. The crisis for him is one of creativity, and in his own view point, the few shinning elements in long poems and the struggles initiated and fabricated by the poet would not lure the reader, and he would end up being the only loser. In "Searching for Nirmana with Smart Fingers", Al-Shafiey succeeded to defeat the coldness of the poetic scene and to reshape its forms to serve its essence depending on huge expressive energy, a power that evolves from the mysteries to which the reader is driven.

The rich and varied implications with their authenticity and uniqueness, have attracted the reader in special ways that were emphasized by a keen alert to all the details. The Robot tells us that "he is by no means a poet of carnivals, neither is his poem a sonic phenomenon" as he is the eternal seeker of the lost keys, some of which he has found with Nirmana, or Nirma, or Nirmala, his lost humanity.

Al-Shafiey has done a lot of travelling to destinations with no cardinal directions, while rejecting to use a compass, unless it it's a magnetic one.

It is no wonder that his poetic collection "Searching for Nirmana with Smart Fingers" has been selected to be taught at the Iowa University in the United States as being a unique prototype of the Arabic prose poem, and we are waiting for the second volume entitled "Laughing Gases". We do not know if Nirmana will cast her shadows on that second volume; we really hope so on an inward level. We have loved her, as well as the skill with which he has crafted the poem for her.

"You say you melt at my truthfulness.

How can I describe myself if I suppose your actual existence at my wakeup and sleep."

"Al-Shafiey Launches (The Complete Collection of a Robot) Into the Horizons of Poetry"
(Article by Egyptian Writer and Journalist Taha Jibreel)

The poet Sharif Al-Shafiey is currently preparing to launch his second part of his poetic collection "The Complete Collection of a Robot" entitled "Laughing Gases" after the enormous success that has been realized by the first volume "Searching for Nirmana with Smart Fingers", and that has been recently chosen to be taught to the students of the Creative Writing Department at Iowa University in the United States, as being a vital and unique added value to the Arabic prose poem.

Al-Ahram Daily quoted Al-Shafiey as saying that the new volume of "Laughing Gases" intended to be published soon reflects, in the first place, the breakaway of man from his humanity, and attempts to depict the traits of our age that can be described as mechanically rich and spiritually poor through a number of condensed scenes. This volume seems to reflect higher momentums, and seems to be simpler than the first volume, composed of 527 poetic sections narrated by the rebelling Robot.

Throughout these scenes, the Robot expresses varied and interrelating human conditions. The first condition is one of pain "The camp of licorice within the molar of the electronic mind"Which would lead to the attempts of searching for remedy or a pain killer. After that comes the state of anesthesia or inhalation of gases causing the bones of the jaws to stretch, drawing a plastic smile colored with medical cotton whiteness on the face, added to unemotional contact with the other sterilized visitors. Following these two conditions, Al-Shafiey says, comes the state of coma, that results from excessive inhalation of laughing gases with implications of hallucinations and the dreams including those of the robot who aspires to get rid of ready-made programs, just as he aspires to get back to his clay from.

These states are concluded by the death condition, which represents a victory of man's free will on the forced-life equipment in hospitals. It is noteworthy that the experience of "The complete Collection of a Robot" represents what can be described as the vital biological adventure within the track of the Arabic prose poem, that is currently in need to new bloods and pulses. In this experience, the

Robot acts as man's agent in doing the talking and the drawing of the poetic scene, where he draws a panoramic image of his hollowness and depressions in the digital age and technical oppressions.

All of this is an attempt to hunt down the essence of objects and relationships, and finally, getting to reunite with the forgotten self. Throughout the text, the Robot expresses his rebellion, and declares his break up with the herd of robots "Humans", and goes on from one scene to the other attacking all colonization powers, sliding over all issues taken for granted and all programmed objects, creating a sustained shake of laws, and revolting against operating and stereo typing systems, with the aim of revealing the truth about a life doomed by calculations, materialism and frames, with fresh nostalgia to his free will and his lost soul outside the equipped universal chamber.

The text represents fresh human thoughts and sophisticated philosophy with a wonderful natural style combing within all the techniques of natural poetry and the achievements of the age, with the World Wide Web at the front lines.

This work by Al-Shafiey is regarded as one of very few works that have spread widely over the past few months through excessive critical reviews, media discussions and distribution chances, thanks to a unique poetic experience that represents a cross roads point between paper and digital creativity. The experience tackles the techniques and components of the age and its new modern language simply and naturally without losing track of depth and vision of the philosophy of "Reviving Man's Humanity" in the age of globalization and submission to materials and technology. This in particular is the essential difference and benchmark between Al-Shafiey and other imitators, who have superficially quoted from the technology and internet terminology resulting in shallow writing.

One other point of strength to be added to the achievement of Al-Shafiey is that he produced his work while being away from his country, as he has been living in Saudi Arabia for three years, cast away from friends and groups. This mood of freedom and independence has had a positive effect on the poet, resulting in huge numbers of followers and readers, along with many critics studying his works from all over the Arab world describing it as being "A white revolt against the Arab poetry", "A state of mobility in the cultural scene", "A vital jump towards the prose poem" and a "Revolution urging free poetry pioneers to revolt".

"An Interesting and Thrilling Experience"
(Critical Review by Egyptian Critic Dr Adel Badr)

In the poetic volume "Searching for Nirmana with Smart Fingers" by the poet Sharif Al-Shafiey, which is the fresh volume among a large project that the poet chose to entitle as "The Complete Collection of a Robot", the Robot functions as the narrator using the digital language of "Zero" and "One", and in particular the language of the machine , the language of the creative individual of robots / humans, and who has ambitions in downplaying concepts and causing a revolution at least on the levels of discovery, logic and writing.

The volume contains 200 internet searches to hunt an extinct creature, thus being a pioneering work in the field, representing the attempts of man to regain himself, and to find his extinct self and Nirmana with her varied names, and he ends up destroying and revealing the ugliness of the false civilization, and tearing the web through an un-flowery poetic style. The volume is located in around 230 pages of the big size, with a mechanical design, big enough for the "Smart Fingers of the Robots", and the symbols of the World Wide Web.

This seems to be in harmony with the content of the experience written by a creative Robot, who rebels against all restrictions, engineering facts and mathematical rules. In reference to the title which is the theme of the work, or its starting point, we find out that it is basically centered on that "human hunting down and searching for Nimana, Nirma, Tita, Nirmala, or Nirvala or any other state of highness and grace, to which this deprived being longs. Such a title could be a summary of the main message in the "Complete Collection of a Robot".

It can also be viewed as a question mark raising inquiries about the nature and issue of the poem's message. The cover also poses a lot of questions, and reveals a lot about the content, as the focus seems greater on an expressive image of the Robot fingers that take the greatest part of the book cover, as designed by the Lebanese designer Patrick Tarabiyah. The design of the hand combines between human hands and, with veins, arteries and nerves made of wires, while the black forefinger, thumb and the middle fingers hold a colorful glowing ball, the globe. At the bottom of the cover design, lies a page screen image of a "yahoo" search with the search for Nimana resulting in "No results can be found for Nimana".

Starting from the dedication phrase to the "Musty Air that forced me to open the window", we log onto that world stuffed with rituals and simple details giving motion to the text. At this point, a question shall be asked about how far is that text harmonious? First, there is no text that is harmonious or not in itself independently from the reader / the recipient. On the contrary, it is the reader who judges the text as being harmonious or not. The theme of the text can be viewed as harmonious in accordance with the readers' understanding of it. Every text that can be understood and interpreted can be considered as harmonious and vice-versa. Through the analysis of Al-Shafiey's Robot collections, a number of points arise:

1-The strong presence of narration throughout the text, which is a phenomenon that deserves contemplation, as there are narrative sentences that take their poetic beauty from the new constructions they are given or through the way they are fitted in and used in the context.
The foolish magnet,
Which insists on considering me iron dust,
Will never win my golden bran.

2-The mobilization of details without excessive and unnecessary decorations, as he logs onto the text and tackles it from the view point of the flowing cinematic narration.
Just like you are summoned easily in my conscience
(Which is not grammatically justifiable),
On the back of a pacified elephant,
So you seep easily into the pores of my cracked skin.
Resorting to this language combines the self with the other partner "Nirmana" or any of her other names. This care for daily life details is a way of getting rid of pure prophetic language, where poetic aspects spring from the context.

3-Each of these texts can be viewed as a cinematic shot, giving reigns to man's views. The narration of the state, here, is the center of the text. In the first text, the search for astonishment prevails as he fails the driving test aboard
I have been driving my car for ten years
So skillfully that roads have envied me!

The surprise which hugged me tight
Is that I have failed the driving test abroad!
At this point we shall note that the text/ cinematic shot, a circular visual text, uses a language close to cinematic scripts through present tense verbs, penetrating the poetic self.

At the next Olympic,
Maybe I'll have a gold medal
In the game of love
After I have been well-trained
To overcome all the runners in the marathon
To embrace the kind Nirmana first

It is not really good
To stand smiling on the tripartite podium
Among two other leopards
I know that they were able to embrace her before.

4-Narration of the inner world that aspires for new discoveries.
Though I didn't get the license,
I felt indescribably happy,
For I have been trained to drive myself
On exceptional errands.

The text gets rid of conventional rhetoric, as it does not suit the Robot anymore. What suits it is breaking away from flowery and decoration language by breaking it which suits the experience.

5-Mysticism of some texts for the sake of breaking away from the motion of regular life, which functions as a pass permit to the other through un-witnessed worlds

I asked her:
"Who are you?"

She said:
"I am myself."

She asked me:
"Who are you?"

I said:
"I am you."

"Searching for Nirmana With Gold Fingers"
(Article by Moroccan Writer and Critic Abdelmounem Chentouf)

Approaching the poetic experience of the Egyptian poet with swimming into his poetic horizons open to adventure with consequences of the disappearance of the smiles of probability, discovery and astonishment.

Since poetry in one of its beautiful definitions is seen as a type of creativity through language and imagination of possible worlds characterized by self-highness and disregard for the daily reality with its obligations and common roles, the real beauty in this text is represented in the poetic treatment of the daily realities' glossary, with consequences of creating a distance between him and the self.

All through the poems of this volume, the reader confronts a deep state of exile giving reigns for a semi-complete paradox between the daily reality clearly symbolized by the Robot, and a potential world, whose spaces the poet has been keen on furnishing with a burning poetic lust, with Nirmana standing as its icon.

Sharif Al-Shafiey is considered one of the Egyptian poets pioneering the contemporary poetic scene. The first volume of his poetic collection of a Robot entitled "Searching for Nirmana with Smart Fingers", his fourth poetic production.

Can we view the preference of the poet to dedicate the book to the "Musty air that forced him to open the window" an introduction to understanding the poem, or a clue that integrates with other ones to reach an interpretation as harmonious and integrated as the text? The opening and closing pairs indicate her presence as an introduction of the Robot and Nirmana to the virtual readers.

This is because the Robot moves, breathes and performs his daily rituals that are characterized by boredom within closed horizons subject to the breaks of limits and fences, while the other (Nirmana) breaks down all fences and ridicules highly raised beings, and spreads her own being to the strong winds of freedom. If the Robot is a personification of steadiness and motionlessness, and lifeless practices, Nermana is the symbol of the movement, mutation, evasion and escape from any limits or restriction.

Faced with Nirmitta's stubborn insistence
On playing a game of ping pong with the Globe,
I was forced to agree!

It was so easy for her
To swat the Globe over the net
From her field to mine,
For she does not believe at all in boundaries
Between the two hemispheres of the table,
And for she played...for the sake of playing.

It is clear in this context that the text introduces Nirvana or Nirmita as being a manifestation of freedom in its utmost from. Nothing proves this representation better than the poetic scene in which she plays "ping pong" with the globe, raising the desire to break down and sieve the structures of morals and tradition to the most. Since this desired freedom resembles strong winds floating above the closed horizons and their ready-made natures, it becomes a state that can never be limited or restrained. As a result, the reader notices the variety of the names given to that icon, as she is Nirmana, as indicated by the title, as well as Nirmeta, Nirma, Nita, Mita, Tita, Nirmala, Nirvala, Noon, and Nona

This icon being a virtual and fairy being, leads to a dream with consequences of chaos, noises, adventure and oppressed desires
The telephone knows she's speaking,
So it is embarrassed at being inoperative,
And throbs so lively that
My nerve wires cannot tolerate!

Nirmana, or Nirma, conveys her presence throughout the poem in this volume as being a disinfectant or a purifier the poet resorts to for ridding himself of his daily routines with sour smells and steady habits. Since the poet is keen on finding her, revelations of her nature keep flowing, deepening the poet's understanding of the ugliness of his daily life, and then his courage to reveal further elements of such ugliness doubles.

Throughout the text the poet conducts a bold and worm dialogue with Nirmana and her multiple masks. In this context, she overflows him with wills or revelations that deepen his feelings of exile from the world of reality, doubling the administrated dozes of purification.

There is the desire to live in the potential world with consequences of the need to create a poetic existence. The reader comes to find out that Nirmana is not a representation of a woman or a female, as the poet tried to convey with extraordinary cleverness, but rather a representation of the poem being regarded as a potential world and a sweet dream that ends with the nightmare of reluctantly returning to the real world. Being accustomed to darkness, as the poet says, ends with little vision, while repeated exposure to Nirmana's rays leads to the confirmed end of permanent inability to view the daily reality and its details.

In that context, then, the fingers that write with ink or click on the key- board, function as agents of the eye in performing the stealthy and transitory realization of Nirmana and her sisters. This provides clear proofs that the dream of permanent residence in the universe of the poem or Nirmana ends with failure. This is because the power of the assumption is always depicted as being fragile and seizing in front of the obligations of daily reality.
The final caftan,
Which my beloved one called "wall calendar" took off
Defeated me hugely
As it reminded me of 365 days of failure
On which I tried to hunt naked Nirmana.

Al-Shafiey has vanished in his adventures with the innovative poetry of potentiality with the necessary rooting of the features of openness, variety and confusion.
Since this poetic gamble has been related to a creature about to become extinct, which is Nirmana, the forms of reaching it varied, with the value of the poem revealed as being able to remove dust away off our daily existence. The moral that the Robot and Nirman are communicating here is that man needs to breathe poetry in the age of Robots and digital fingers.

The Complete Collection of a Robot (1)
SEARCHING FOR NIRMANA WITH SMART FINGERS
(By Sharif Al-Shafiey)

<u>**Search 1**</u>

I have been driving my car for ten years
So skillfully that roads have envied me!

The surprise which hugged me tight
Is that I have failed the driving test abroad!

The cop told me that
I had gazed at the mirror.
I answered that I was in fact not to blame:
Nirmana was sitting on the back seat!

Though I didn't get the license,
I felt indescribably happy,
For I have been trained to drive myself
On exceptional errands.

Search 2

I asked her:
"Who are you?"

She said:
"I am myself."

She asked me:
"Who are you?"

I said:
"I am you."

Waves overwhelmed Nirmana; she yelled at me:
"Keep to your flat;
Turn off the water clasp quickly!"

Search 3

Just like you are summoned easily in my conscience
(Which is not grammatically justifiable),
On the back of a pacified elephant,
So you seep easily into the pores of my cracked skin.
My interconnected atoms soak you up,
My atoms which are eager to be soluble
Into quicklime.

You com your hair irritably before me,
While I quietly press the keys of the computer keyboard.
I write the letters of your name in the search engine "Yahoo":
Nirmana
Nirma
Nirmitta
Nitta
Mitta
Titta
Nirmala
Nirvana
Nirva
Noreena
Noritta
Narmitta
Narmina
Nermina
Noon
Nona
N

The screen answers back with a smile
Like ships' projectiles
With two wings and a tail,
Yet unable to fly.

Sixteen zeros hover over my head in the room
0000
0000
0000
0000

To the beak of each zero is a piece of my
Hemisphere
(All with the appropriate diacritics).

Out of my warty embarrassment I make a balloon.
I fly with it up to the older planet in the galaxy,
Where no one clips their pretty nails,
With which they cut their life's way through
And dig their graves.

Search 4

The hearth and incense odour
Coming from the neighbours' pleased me.
I preferred to delay frying the fish till the evening,
For the dispersed oil not burn
A stray butterfly inside my bosom.

I expected an exquisite dream that night,
Especially after I had decided to sleep without dining
And without cover.

Indeed,
Nirmitta broke the cocoon,
And kept on flexing her neck coquettishly many a time,
While I was giving her an enthusiastic clap!

Search 5

I am in no need to conquer the space
For I already possess over a thousand satellite channels
In my bedroom.
(Perhaps these satellite channels are those
Who possess and imprison my humanness
With all its successive phases).

I am still in need of conquering Nona
And plunging into her tissues in a spacesuit,
After the dish and the decoder have failed
In dealing with her nearby, strong signals!

Search 6

The telephone knows she's speaking,
So it is embarrassed at being inoperative,
And throbs so lively that
My nerve wires cannot tolerate!

Nirvana
"Good morning" from her lips is so sufficient for me to ask:
"How shall I bear with my human odour
After I've been immersed in angelic perfume?!"

"Nice dreams" from her eyes are so fit for me to implant the
delicious virus in my electronic exhausted mind
And erase my valid and invalid cells.

Why did Nirvana not appear
In the digital photo I took of her?
Do I really own a telephone?

Search 7

Faced with Nirmitta's stubborn insistence
On playing a game of ping pong with the Globe,
I was forced to agree!

It was so easy for her
To swat the Globe over the net
From her field to mine,
For she does not believe at all in boundaries
Between the two hemispheres of the table,
And for she played…for the sake of playing.

As for me,
Though I played…for the sake of playing,
I found it difficult to swat the Globe over the net,
For fear of being accused of political "anti-boundarism"
And of being a supporter of global conflicts
With coloured fruit and green leaves
And scary dark shadows.

Search 8

With a wet cloth,
I clean my mirror,
Except for the free-moving magnetic arrow on my brow
And the buttons of my surpriseproof coat!

I clench and stretch my fist many a time.
I open and close my mouth many a time.
I count my teeth, not uncertain about their number,
Only for feeling relieved that I am
The kind—nay, very kind friend of numbers,
Who does not harm anyone,
Nor wants to wound himself ever,
Even if he has shattered the mirror with his clenched fist
And preferred gazing at his dark shadow on the
Rough wall,
Much like Nirmana.

Search 9

The pillow has announced
That it won't be able to keep my head on till the morning.

This was in response to an anaesthetic injection I took
To be ready to chuck the extra tongue in my mouth,
Which utters incomprehensible words
All beginning in any of the following five letters:
N.I.R.M.A.

Thank God!
There is no risk to the epiglottis
Since it is dumb.

Search 10

I was not sufficiently attentive
Perhaps because of back pains
Which have increased with long periods of sitting
At office and at home.
So, my finger erred in punching the keyboard:
I wrote "normal" instead of "Nirmala".
Upon this, the search engine Yahoo smiled excessively
passionately.
All world's women visited me on that night.
All coloured birds caressed my brain gently.

It was really embarrassing
To yawn many a time,
Or sleep
Before distributing the sweets to my guests,
Though generosity is among my hereditary chromosomes!

Search 11

I did not believe Nirmana when she whispered:
"Your eyes say many things."
= "My eyes or my glasses?"
"Your eyes behind your glasses."
= "What does my nose say then?!"
"It says you've been addicted to inhaling absurdities!"
= "What did my good eyes tell you?"
"That you know well I am nonexistent!"
= "Ha...ha...ha..."

Search 12

I walked barefoot on stones and nails
From midnight to morning
Without any personal will
Or any desire to imitate Nirmana,
Or as some thought,
Or as I thought.

The absurd fact
Is that I have perforce been committed to the market rules,
As all shoes shops and all shops
Were to open and close
At strictly observed times.

Search 13

With the whiff of the first summer breeze,
I moved my warm clothes to the remotest point in my wardrobe,
Turning a deaf ear to the meteorologists' warnings
About weather changes.

I rearranged the whole wardrobe.
I gazed at my military suit for a long time,
Not knowing where to put it indeed.
Shall I get rid of it?
I do not think I will get a formal summons.
"We are not in a state of war,"
At least as morning newspapers
And news briefs say.

Strangely, I selected the best hook
And hung the military suit on
In the nearest point in the wardrobe,
Only to sleep soundly,
Certain that no one will dare steal my wife's jewellery
From the upper shelf.

When I slept afterwards,
I dreamt of running in the scorching sun,
Clad in a helmet and military boots only,
Carrying a machine gun.

I tried to kill stray dogs,
Which forced Nirmina to collect her sheep
And to leave her wooden cottage on the mountain.
I fired the bullets in vain.
All dogs melted in fortresses and troughs.

I woke up tired.
I found the thieves had completely destroyed the wardrobe.
The jewellery was intact...Thank God!
Yet sons of a bitch had stolen my military suit.
Did they covet the hook?!

Search 14

Nirma's message hit my e-mail inbox:
"Eat well and sleep well
To give me a hearty welcome in the morning."

Immediately I repeated:
"The hair fixer does not fit your lineaments tonight.
Food and sleep are outcast from my room
Till you come, hungry and red-eyed."

Why did her unsigned message remind me
Of the tawdry deodorant
Which gave me a rash?

Search 15

I dreamt a lot
Of having broken the world record in pole-valuting

I dreamt a lot of the pole
Being broken beneath me
And falling on her dead body.

I asked Nirmana:
"Which dream did you admire more?"
She quietly said:
"My dreams of becoming a pole
Which upped me to the sky
Then broke beneath me."

Search 16

I was not so mad
As to shun, alone, the Titanic movie,
The one which excessively passionately embraced many cultures
from all the corners of the globe,
Pretending to heal its fractured bones.

I was not so stable
As to embrace, alone, the Titanic show,
Which had penetrated me like a bullet,
Pretending to disinfect me
Through phlebotomizing and cupping.
Against the toxicants of the world's cultures
And against evil spirits.

Search 17

The history inside me
Is eaten up by geography.

The geography inside me
Is bitten by history.

The difference between Nirvana and Miss Universe 2007
Is that the latter is geography laid into history,
While Nirvana
Is a history refusing to be laid upon any geography.

Search 18

In the old, run-down temple,
Which had been renovated by engineers in 48 hours using ready-
made walls,
Technology went up the pulpit,
Holding a rosary.
Then, the beads of the congregation slipped apart
And everyone missed the prayer-direction.

All alone,
I kept on prostrating myself, in my room, to the Deity,
In sheer reverence,
Wishing that Nirmana's words,
Which she often repeats but I do not understand,
Mean "God be exalted!"

Search 19

Nirmitta's live and extinguished flames
Are not done by my match, nor by my water.

I only own one match,
Hoarding it up for a day of electricity outage,
When I should look at myself quickly,
Then drink all the water I have.

Search 20

The heart's clock wishes
To mistake the time one time,
To ring two at 1 o'clock prompt!

This does not mean I desire two women
— God forbid!
God be my witness, I am jaded of women.
It is all about
That I would like to assure Nirmana
That the planets of the galaxy and the electrons of the atom
Might not regularly rotate.

Search 21

"Is the old towel
Suitable for absorbing my new sweat?
Is my sweat really free from chemically equivalent salts, and has
the taste of hot spices?!"

Thus did I ask Nirmana,
So she stuck a medical plaster to her lips.

Search 22

Test tubes,
An anatomy set,
A white coat,
A white rat.
The heart should be white to conduct the experiment!
Yet my goal, I swear to God, is so noble:
I want to observe what exactly happens to living tissues
When injected with Nirma's nectar
And when injected with its absence.

Nirma refused to help me conduct the experiment,
Pretending that she does not recognize ant rat
Other than me.

Search 23

I do usually not take pleasure at the circus,
For monsters remind me of myself,
Which has turned monstrous despite me.
The hard acrobatics do not attract an acrobat like me,
Who daily walks tight ropes
And dances with the moon, snakes and smokes.

What really astonished me in the last show
And Nirmana described as "Horrifying"
Is the episode of lions on the rampage,
Which suddenly pounded at their trainer.
Instead of snapping or trying to finish him off,
They whipped him
And asked him to jump nimbly through the fire circle,
For he is the new hero of the great taming epic,
The one deserving survival and standing ovations.

Search 24

The Coke tin …to the red fridge:
"You're surely not my mother."

The gum to the teeth:
"I wish I had a tongue to stick out at you."

Rubbish…to the dustbin:
"If anyone had accepted you, I wouldn't have."

I to Nona:
"My placenta is connected to you, giving me some of your glow.
You chew me, so I wish to taste you with my tongue.
The "noon" of the feminine marker has accepted me, but I accept
only Nona."

Search 25

With Noreena's cap
I only feel warm, but I do not disappear.
(Who said her cap is the 'vanishing cap'?!)

Without Noreena's cap
I can tolerate cold,
Especially in crowded places,
But certainly no one sees me!

Search 26

The cinema was not complete;
40% of the seats were vacant.
Most of the spectators felt the film was dull
After less than half an hour.

The hero is jobless.
He refuses bribery
To land a job opportunity.
He thinks his father's fortune anathema to him.
His father is implicated in corruption and money laundering cases.
He smokes since childhood
In third-rate cafes.
He is addicted to politics in fake partisan dens.
His life, in general, is not subject to any pragramme.

The heroine, who feigns romanticism,
Measures her dreams with a tape-measure.
She prefers boiled food, and sleeps early.
She smiles cautiously on familial occasions.
She removes her headscarf at beaches and in wedding parties
In a classic attempt to hunt down a legible suitor.

When the hero fell in her snares,
The spectators despised the plot.
He did not desire her,
Nor did she see him in the first place!

I wished then
To watch a more realistic or interesting film
About famines,
About racial discrimination,
About terrorist blasts,
Even about genocide.

On the next day,
I went to the Greco-Roman Theatre.
Nirmana is the sole heroine, as I was told.
"Legal Conquer" is the title of the play.
Nirmana did not stop at conquering my bodily cells,
But managed to steal the secrets of the soul.
I acknowledge her real cleverness.

Several weeks later, she told me:
"I'll leave on 2/9/2007
And will never come back."

My vocal cords were unable to vibrate.
I importuned her in every possible way to recant.
She insisted on fulfilling her wish,
Brushing away my incessant attempts.

I said:
"It's my absence…not yours."
She burst into laughter, and in an exuberant voice, said:
"You've failed the emotion- suppression exam,
And I've succeeded in the rehearsals of my new play!"

Before quarrelling with her,
Due to her extreme insipidity,
She said in an inimitable voice:
"Forgive me…I'm really a bitch!"

Search 27

Life's fits sometimes shake me up;
They do not stop except through overdoses
Of appropriate "humanicides".

My major problem with Noreena
Is that she blesses my rise from hibernation,
While I fear living in her sunny orchard
More than five minutes.

Being accustomed to darkness
Usually ends in some visibility.
Yet being accustomed to Noreena's rays
Has a certain end:
Not being able to see anymore.

Search 28

Eventually, I managed to possess a cheque book.
But I still do not have a "signature"
Or a distinctive fingerprint.

The cheques drawn by Nirmana to me
Were in no need to a signature from her:
Her handwriting is unprecedented.
More important for me than cashing these cheques
Is to keep them as souvenirs.

Search 29

The brain CAT scan has clearly shown
That there are no cells infected with Nirma's Syndrome.

The cardiograph
Asserts uneven beats with no clear reason.

The body's electricity
Seems strangely more than usual.

The blood analysis
Indicates the percentage of chlorophyll.

The speculum
Has captured photos of a bride and groom in the honeymoon.

The sexual potency test
Asserts my uniqueness in pumping valid jasmine seeds
Into any soil
With no chemical fertilizers.

The lie detector
Has given warning signals.
When I was asked about Nirma, I said:
"She's the mirage."

Search 30

Whenever I eat a piece of Nirmana,
Or cut a slice from her with the scissors,
I feel guilt-ridden.
But this feeling soon vanishes when
Nirmana stands on the scale
Finding that her weight has increased.

This has encouraged me
To search for a supermarket
Selling goods growing for me with consumption!

Search 31

The games I have learnt alone are so many,
The most important of which are:
The fierce bullfighting within my lean body;
Performing acrobatics dexterously
On the parallel bars of life;
And duelling the scarecrow
Which has occupied my mirror.

Nirmitta has taught me more dangerous games,
But more interesting.

She has taught me rhythmical dancing with fish.
In the bed of the lake,
And throwing explosive conches at fishermen
When trying to come closer.
(The sea Nirmitta with fins
Considers eating fish an unforgivable sin.)

She has taught me to imitate the humans I like
And tame animals
In a caricature fashion, exposing their cruel shortcomings.

She has taught me singing in the morning
Even with a wooden, chinked pharynx.

Nirmitta has made me accustomed
To taking intensive doses
Of spiritual amphetamines.
I have loved this too much.
I have hated thinking of my state after having become an addict.
I find new packets.
(They are natural extracts
Not sold in pharmacies ipso facto.)

Nirmitta did not stop at activating visible files
In my hard and floppy disks,
Yet she activated my hidden ones
And even the ones long thrown into the recycle bin.

She also activated my sweat and tear glands.
She said the odour of sweat and the glow of tears
Increase men's attractiveness.

She described herself as mad,
And moved her horoscope behind my skewed horoscope.

She knowingly insisted
On playing hide and seek with me.
This was, of course, against my will.
With the whistle blow,
It knowingly made clear to me
That everything had ended.

Search 32

Credibility will cease
When I sign any protocol
To reduce environmental pollution,
For my hand itself is extremely polluted!

Luck will replace credibility
When it transpires that the lottery paper in my drawer
Is Nirmana herself
As the lottery-seller has promised me,
The one with a polluted conscience!

Search 33

The room is empty of maquettes, paintings
And definitely visitors.
Yet in the middle of it was a vainglorious painter
Who claimed that he was the only one
Capable of compressing all void
Into four walls.

The international award
Given to our fellow
Ensures my credibility,
For I have been claiming for a thousand years
That I am the only one
Capable of compressing Nirmana
Inside Recalcitrance House,
Regardless of who obeys who?

Search 34

In the Special Aptitude Test,
I was asked:
"When is happiness measured in barrels?"

The answer which proved my ingenuity was:
"When Nirvana is extracted from oil wells."

Search 35

The world with seven wonders
Covets the eighth.

I, the one with one "noon" (i.e. whale),
Do not covet except one wonder.
Every morning, the "noon" swallows me,
So I recite: "There is no god but thou: glory to thee: I was indeed
wrong!"(2)

---

² See surat Al Anbeyya'; the Holy Qur'an, *021.087.*

Search 36

The DNA tests did not disprove
That Nirmana's baby
Of the two dimples and long fingers
Is my seed out of a legitimate relationship.

Tests did not disprove that
Nirmana herself
Is the oldest brainchild
Out of an illegitimate relationship.

Search 37

Seven lions, and I am the eighth,
Have concurred on betrayal.

I asked the deficient language about what to do.
It answered I am, in the case of fulfilling my promise,
Required to break it!
When not fulfilling it,
I am required to fulfil it!

Nirmana
Described all mortals, treaties and words
As mad circles,
Where fulfilment and betrayals
Are the same,
And asked me to await her forever
At the central point.

Search 38

The coastal city
Has never thought of betraying the sea.
However,
The sea has been very angry with her,
Since she did not immerse herself completely into it.

I am not allowed to betray.
Based on this skewed logic,
I am not also allowed to betray betrayal!

When Archimedes set the Floating Law,
Nirmana laughed heartily
And dived into the deep blue sea against the "centrifugal"
To prove to scientists that the "law" is "betrayal".

Archimedes in turn laughed, saying:
"Nirmana is indeed the most truthful lie!"

Search 39

The radioactive metal Niranium
Is not included in the periodical table of chemical elements.

It is my discovery,
And no one believes its existence except for me.

Perhaps because I am the only one
Who fell victim of its fissure reactions.

Perhaps because I am the only chemist worldwide
Or perhaps because I am the only one
Who does not know anything about chemistry.

Search 40

The robots mutinant against their essential laws
Which control their movements(3)
Have tempted me to desperately defend my existence as a human
Even if it would lead to disgrace with humans
Or cause them harm
Directly or indirectly.

The "zero" law which Nirvana set for me
And acknowledged is not binding.
It stipulates the following:
= The only person who believes in
Nirvana may not harm her, nor allow any harm to her.
= This person shall obey Nirvana's orders, unless this runs counter
to the first stipulation.
= This person shall preserve his existence so long as this does not
run counter to the first and second stipulations.

---

[3] The basic laws of the robots emerged for the first time in 1942 in a
science fiction by the Russian-American novelist Isaac Asimov. These laws
support the well-being of robots provided they obey human commands and
do not cause them harm.

Search 41

Nirmana does not believe I have become world-famous
Just I own an accredited visa card,
An international license,
And a passport with stamps of 21 countries,
Between them and us
Are good relations
Or reconciliation and peace treaties.

Nirmana asserts
That the smell of the hot oil in my mouth
(I mean "saliva")
Cannot be obliterated with American mint,
And that the callous in my foot
Cannot be covered in Italian shoes
Made of deluxe genuine leather.

Nirmana (despite everything)
Believes in my private property (in everything),
In a cloak of "Mrs Ghost",
Where no one except for me can ever see her,
Not even the director of a fantasy movie,
The sole hero of which is me.

Search 42

The most beautiful feeling in the world
Is for a model rose to grant me her perfumed blood,
Which is the top possibility for a Dracula like me,
And is the most cherished dream for other humans.

The most wondrous thing about the rose impossible,
Nirva,
With the compound paraphernalia,
Is that it sprinkles her unique blush at me,
And I take pleasure at my suffering,
Where I have no clean bottle,
In which I keep
That sealed nectar.

Search 43

The greatest miracle of Nirvana
Is that she awakens he who is awake,
And yawns before the sleeper to sleep.

Perhaps she is very ordinary,
But is able to make usual people miracle-workers.

In the last chat with her, for example,
After a few hours
Of eating a pizza together at the beach
And sipping the moisture mixed with pungent iodine
My words turned into some kind of improvised poetry,
Though I suffer from speaking
And difficulty with smithing words not used in
Logic books.

In less than five minutes, I told her
Those cane sugar injected statements:
"I watched you today performing a human action called 'eating', so that
I made sure that quasi-angels eat, not as I spread the word. As for me, your taste
is enough for me: any food may disturb my five senses.
"When I meditated your bright smiling face,
I envied myself much for owning the sun alone, after I had left the city for hours.
Many a time I wished to see the sea yell at us, and order to put on his garment together, for eyes to forget us, and for eyelids to remember us, while we are hiding in one chance roomy enough for us.
"You are not dots on my letters. You are my new alphabet, through which I understood the whole world. When I uttered them, no one understood me. It is enough for me that you can move my tongue, even though you do not side with its language.
"What you are hearing now is not my voice, nor my muteness. It is the clicking of my iron being with your electrical energy drawn from lightning. My machine operates despite me, believe me, after your waves have been connected to you. What I fear is to work nonstop, and I cannot control it or stop working at will, so that I cannot control my life.
You are the acting one, not the actress.

You are the fountain of art which is poured out to be worked out of its own accord. The director, photographer and workers are all nothing but your audience, who cannot help clapping for you. I am the one who is angry at his fate, for I have two days only to clap for you.

Today, I wished to split like amoeba thousand times to fulfil the wish of a people all of its sects wished to circumambulate you.

"I exist through you; that is how I understand, not heeding names. You are yourself, and names do not concern me. You are growing inside me, though the area of your chart is much bigger than my skin. My pregnancy is not false, believe me. I contain you, but you also contain me, believe me, and none of us has a cover.

"Only today did I smell the madness

Emitted from your tobacco, so I lived one thousand nights. What if I hugged madness and sucked its nectar into my run-down heatproof intestines? After burning your tobacco, you forgot your firelighter with me, perhaps at your will. I do not want firelighters; if only you left me a fire extinguisher! I advise you to try smoking humans; you will not need firelighters; you will light them with your eyes' fuel and your smiles' triggers.

You say you melt at my truthfulness.

How can I describe myself if I suppose your actual existence at my wakeup and sleep."

Search 44

I said to Nirmana:
"You're the granite girl,
Who gave me an indulgence
And allowed me to re-sculpt her."

She said to me:
"You are a liar!
I'm immutable and un-renamble.
You're sure not a sculptor,
And can cleans yourself with Dettol."

Search 45

Obtaining the minimum
Clarity of the relationship between me and Nirmana
Requires building a huge inter-network
Connecting my access points to hers.

More important than the absence of censorship
On the network
Is for the time distance between my beginning and end
To be longer than the time information flow takes
Between my points and hers.

Search 46

The shoe Cinderella forgot at the party
Was not enough
To search for the stray spectre
Hiding in a cave
On the outskirts of the city.

The footprints of Nirmina's bare feet
On the granite of my spirit
Were enough
For congregating for an interesting shuttle journey
To search for her flesh and blood in the world continents
Or at least to make sure for the earth to remain globular
Like the ball of fire in my throat.

Search 47

I have not laughed for long time
Like I did last night
In the charity party
I gave my at my elegant house
For the victims of Alzheimer,
Who were unable to remember their real names
Or even forget their missing fingers.

I laughed a lot indeed
When Nirmitta pulled
My colourful bow-tie
And kept on dragging me round the dinner table,
And I was gasping behind her, looking eagerly at the dishes.

Nirmitta innocently asked me
About the secret of my hysterical happiness.
I earnestly said:
"Don't you see their missing fingers
Having safely returned and filled dishes?!"

Astonished, she gazed at me and muttered in surprise:
"It's just the deluxe shrimps you like!"
Then, I realized I had been seized by seasickness.
I burst into asking amnesic people while swaggering:
"Which one is the Captain?
I want this ship
To return to the coast immediately."

Search 48

Behind Nirmala who is extending before me like a screen
I clearly see life and death on the stage
Swapping seats and roles,
And myself approaching myself in quickened paces.

Is Nirmala that transparent,
Or is she nonexistent?

Search 49

Since I feel that attraction to Nirmala
And rotating her
More hazardous than dealing in weapons
And planting poppy,
I suggested including the following article
In the International Declaration on Human Rights:
"Every person has the right everywhere to
Freedom of believing in Nirvana's existence
And freedom of expressing that belief
Through public practice."

In the crossword puzzle
Are all the abstruse questions.
I answered them as follows:

N	I	R	M	A
I				M
R				R
M				I
A	M	R	I	N

Surprisingly,
All my answers were correct.

Search 51

By February 30th,
I will have celebrated the first birthday of Tita.

On April 1st of the same year,
Rumor will have it that I am alive.

At the end of that year,
I will discover that February 30th is imaginary,
And April 1st is the day of trite lies.

Search 52

One trick is left
For priests, quack doctors and caricaturists
Who wish to turn dust into gold.

They only need to mix dust with butter
And legs of boiled chickens,
Then to put the mixture into my boots
To obtain gold,
After I cover 7 kilometers walking barefoot
Provided walking
Is in Nona's direction.

Search 53

I asked the treacherous gloves
About the source of the fatal bacteria
Hidden in their bowels.

They refused to disclose their accomplices
And set fire to themselves to commit suicide,
Fearing I electrocute them with Nirvana
And they die seven hundred thousand times.

Do I need to wash my hand seven hundred thousand times
Before I shake hands with Nirvana?
How many times shall I wash my mouth and teeth
Before kissing her
And biting her unpeeled apple?

Search 54

Those dwelling in skyscrapers
Are much taller than me
(According to the pictures taken by imbecilic satellites).
Despite this,
I do not envy them,
Nor are their abodes secure against earthquakes and winds.

I see them in their real shape.
They only see my virtual lineaments,
Which do not serve their interests
In the other side of the globe.

I am dedicated
To reading my palm and tree leaves.
They do not have time for such readings,
And their palms are not engraved,
And their tree leaves are not green.

My lifelong dream is one pearl conch
And to remain in my delicious coma
Away from mortals' noise and blunders.
They are dead beats
Because they want to collect all world's pearls
Legally and illegally.

I love Nirvana,
And indeed believe in her existence.
They like no one to love no one,
And more important for them
Than denying Nirvana's existence
Is denying anyone who does not deny her existence!

Search 55

In a bee's confessions in the Police Station,
It was reported she is mixing her honey with glucose.

In the flower's confessions in the same station,
It was reported she is mixing her nectar with water.

In my own confessions
At home and under no pressure,
It was reported I am fooling all people,
As I hug them with two arms,
While my true arms are chasing Nona
In the hope of hugging her.

Search 56

Despite my thinness,
The doctor advised me to book two seats for me in the train
After I have become schizophrenic.

I have always to choose:
On which seat should I sit first
While the other seat is vacant, waiting for me.

It is not within my authority
To grant the vacant seat to anyone
Even temporarily.

When I discovered that on my own journey
To Mrs Noreena,
Who was not able to book a seat,
The Railway Authority refused to let her sit.
She was told it was extremely dangerous for her
To approach the seat of an incurable patient.

I related to the doctor what happened.
He quietly and unjustifiably asked me
To leave his clinic and search for another doctor,
Forgoing a huge sum of money I monthly pay him.

Search 57

From a gymnasium hall to another,
I got addicted to moving about
In the hope of enlarging my muscles
Through intensive training
And amino hormones.

Maybe I succeed in tailoring my body
To my cold crystals
Which replaced eyes
For most mortals.

Surely, my soul will remain intact
Until Nirvana blows a natural one from her spirit into it,
Then it will be just my size.

Search 58

The foolish magnet,
Which insists on considering me iron dust,
Will never win my golden bran.

How did Nirmana respond to my call,
Though my ears are nonmagentizable
And the magnetic field of my phraynx is so weak?

Search 59

I have often protested
Against running me from outside,
Not because I am a free man
With will, reason and initiatives,
Nor because I am an egoist being to the extreme.
I prefer sucking my toes
Than using them as dynamites in quarries
Or as sausages in international restaurants
Or even as "Zeinab's fingers"(4) for my children in the feast.

Why did I accept so easily
To be run by Nirvana?
Maybe because she is eager to run me from inside.

---

[4] A well known dessert in Egypt.

Search 60

The able international referee
Carded me the following:

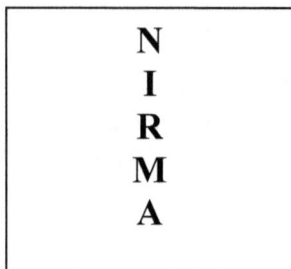

```
N
I
R
M
A
```

I immediately abided by the decision,
Leaving the field politely
Amidst other players', competitors' and spectators' surprise.

After the match, I asked him about the carding;
He said:
"Because you're the one who deserved looking at the card and
winning autism in adulthood."

Search 61

Before lunch:
All the family members are around the table.

On the table:
A huge cock,
Large amounts of rice,
Countless water bottles.

After lunch:
Three people only around the table.
Their hands around their bulgy bellies.
Cutlery is in the empty dishes
Stained with the cock's meat
And with the rest of the family's blood!

In the nearby room:
I made real effort
To convince Nirmana
I am her easy prey.

Search 62

Nirmana thought of making herself a flag
Out of cloth, never tattering nor perishing,
To flutter freely in the air
In the case of confiscating her breath
At the hands of customs officials
Who belong to the past,
Or at the hands of me,
Who belongs to the future.

I thought of putting my picture on a monetary unit
Or even on a stamp
To belong to a particular value
When I lose breath
At the tobacco factory I own.

Search 63

The road from home to the tannery
Means to my trousers
They will regain their original colours forcibly
After being dyed out.

The road from the tannery to home
Told me I am defenseless,
For all my trousers spoke instead of the denim jeans
According to the new tannery's owner.

The most important step in my errand
Is that Nirmana has identified with some of my steps.

Search 64

Titta sympathetically laughed
When I told her I had assigned her
A tone in my mobile suitable for her.
It is certain then
That she did not save my number in her memory.

The astonishing thing
Is that she asked me about the tone.
I half-heartedly answered her:
"His tale is a long one…His story a long one!"

She piqued me when asking to listen to it.
Angrily I said:
"Save my number.
Stand by me and call me to listen to it."

When she did so,
Silence reigned the place,
So I was sure my heart had been out of service.

Search 65

Perhaps Mitta understood why I wept
When I saw a white hair in my beard.

I did not understand why Mitta wept
When she did not find a single white hair in my head.

Search 66

I asked the vacuum cleaner
About the secret behind my misery.
She said:
"Because you overused me
So much so I swept you along!"

I asked Nirmala about the secret behind my misery.
She said:
"Because your watch is overprecise
So much so I failed to be the center of its dial
And to plant the transparent hands in place of the visible ones."

Search 67

My friend noticed
I had pressed "Refresh" in my e-mail page
Around 70 times in one minute.
I did not expect a new message from Nirmana
As he thought.
It was just a reflex
To increase my heart beats
And refresh my frozen blood circulation.

Search 68

Out of the voltage between me and Noritta
An electrical battle,
Hard to measure by voltameter,
Grew.
Its beginning was the marriage registrar's door,
And its end the same door.
Between the commencement and end whistles,
The marriage registrar managed to input my limited data in his book,
And started inputting Nirmana's endless data
In vain.

Search 69

The infant Nona found
At the door of the grand mosque
Was prettier than singly named.

Nona asked me
To help her choose a name for the infant.
I said:
"She's the one with 'noon'
Or with all letters.
I name her inhalation and exhalation:
A filtering of the polluted world.

I name her virginity:
A veto to the ozone hole;
Dialysis of the kidneys of poor country's children.
I name her dignity:
The blacks and Red Indians' victory.
I name her presence:
A denunciation of my presence on the face of the gasping globe
And a landing of your presence."

Search 70

In her solid state,
Nirmana attracts all precious metals.
I have envied my few gold teeth,
Which were uprooted flying to her,
Not heeding the haemorrhage
Nor the void it left in my miserable mouth.

In her liquid state,
Nirmana does not assume the shape of the bowl it occupies.
She does not freeze in coldness.
She does not vaporize out of heat.
She is moody like waves,
Beneficent like flood,
And able to generate electricity
Necessary for lighting a whole city
And electrocuting the greedy in its warm spots.

In her gaseous state,
Nirmana fraternizes with the white-hot iron.
They both roll over my withering heart
Perhaps to eradicate it
Or to receive it.

Search 71

Right after rain-seeking prayers,
Nirmana poured,
So I performed the absent-seeking prayers for myself.

Search 72

One drop of mercurochrome
On my white shirt
Is enough to cure it of idealism.

One drop of shirt
On my skin
Is enough to cure it of primitiveness.

One drop of "N"
On my letters
Is enough to cure them of being read and written.

Search 73

I have learned from a close friend
That the police are planning to arrest Nirmana.
I do not believe that the police are that cruel.
I do not know why I fell to calling out the list of accusations
In unprecedented enthusiasm.

I found myself yelling at people in a public square:
"Nirmana spied on my conscience
For the sake of my twin lost in jungles
Seven thousand years ago."

Nirmana launched coloured aeroplanes.
Very effortlessly, without clasping their threads.
So she annoyed the parliament members,
Businessmen
And new noblemen
While enjoying their private beaches.

Nirmana destroyed fashion halls
And emancipated women of high heels and makeup;
So she sentenced them all to death, skinned
By their foolish husbands' tongues.

Nirmana spat on the face of the commodification civilization.
She kissed my daughter, who dislikes gold, between her eyes.
Nirmana anticipated the end of the Paper Age,
And wrote all this in her memoirs on mud slates.

Nirmana planned a putsch
And hyped up anarchy in family's love rooms
And in virtual chat rooms.

Nirmana planted wheat secretly,
Made bread-dispensing leaves with no leaves,
And distributed them to tramps
And stray cats.

Nirmana chalk-marked
The shirts of weapon-dealers,
Of human appendages
And of those involved in corruption cases.

Nirmana blew herself up with a suicide belt
At the heart of the slaves market teaming with traders,
Then stood up to dance, naked, for slaves
To the rhythms of tabors.

Nirmana made a medicine
For mincing bureaucracy
And burglar alarm
Against moulding brains and stiff necks.

Nirmana melted like a sugar cube
Into the dawn's ears,
Into the ecclesiastical hymns
And into the beauteous sun flowers' nectar.

The truth the public square believes in
Is that Nirmana has never regretted
Any of her actions,
While regert presses me hard
For being accustomed to hitting trees' shades with my car.

Search 74

When Nona sneezed,
Out of her nostrils a woman with a medallion and a tail came,
Who fell to devouring my bosom's withering grass,
And with a small axe,
Reduced my rib cage into rubble.

I wished she could find antiquated coins.
Perhaps I could sell them to smuggling gangs
For a suitable price.
The woman wished to find a bullet
To fire at the faces of state enemies
On my behalf.

When I sneezed,
My tissue paper was torn by force of phlegm.
All fled, fearing the possible infection.
Nona did approach my respiratory system, whispering:
"Bless you!"

Search 75

She hurled flaming stones at my face
When night stars informed her I love her.

Politely, I told her:
"Nirma,
I'm not ready to love you.
Simply because
I'm not ready to love myself."

Search 76

Many a time I listened
To the pieces of advice of the NLP site,
In the hope I discover my internal treasures,
And achieve success in life
Through harnessing the regal force of mind
And reversing the time line.

As soon as the Nirma Programming (NP) site was launched
In the space of neural web,
The secret insurgency cells managed
To depose the king of mind,
And to cast time waves in all directions.
Further, the NLP site was hidden
As a "cheap" site
That does not lead to discovering treasures.

Search 77

In a suit of a veteran warrior
Who lost his arms in the Battle of Normandy,
I steeled myself to going to Nirmana's coasts
On board of a rubber boat
In the smallest naval landing operation in history.

Nirmana is, of course, not a colony to be liberated,
But she is the only chart
That deserves me granting her my limbs willingly
On a gold platter.

Search 78

The only time in her life
In which Nirmana used remote control
Was when switching me off.
That was when I pointed the video gama pistol at her face
And asked her to turn into a prey on the screen
For a femtosecond.

It was a fascinating scene,
For her magic wand swallowed my hallucinations,
And blood trickled out of me slowly
Writing on the ground:"GAME OVER",
While her vague perfume "miracle" spread all over.

(How did "miracle" hog the atmosphere
Although she told me
She had exchanged it for the astonishing Cabotine
Two weeks ago?!)

Search 79

It is totally incomprehensible
To become a tight glowing slot in her agenda
Perhaps because she does not have an agenda,
Perhaps because I am not sufficiently glowing,
Nor that tight.

The truth I got alone
Is that Nitta is the actual rubber of my entire agenda
After she has opened an account for me
In the anarchy bank.

Search 80

When Nirmina spoke,
I missed her silence.
When she fell silent,
I missed her voice.

When she came then disappeared,
Then came then disappeared,
I wished 'then' to be deleted from the alphabet,
For me to plunge into the sand-sea forever
Or to reach the stars, dragged from my mouth by a hook.

When she forgot her flaxen clothes in my room,
I immediately remembered
That my hair had been disheveled some thousand years ago.
I was greatly pleased with her fingerprints on my shirt's sleeve.

Should I give them back to her because she dropped them unawares
And get 10% of her fingers according to the law?
Or should I give them in to the police
As concrete evidence of her being a robber of sleep from my
conscience?
Or should I plant them in a water pot
For lotuses to become queens and top-notch ladies?
Or should I present them to my heart
To become a stringed instrument?
Or leave them on the sleeve
To test the potency of the new washing powder?

Search 81

With Nirmana's continuous fasting,
I have to find a way to conquer her
Other than being her salt.

Search 82

At whom should I take shelter this cold night?
The moon is so close,
But it is the prey of travellers, poets and psychotherapists.

Coats are galore,
But I fear they might eat me out.

Nirvana is present in the blood circulation…extremely,
Yet she is nobler than melting white fats
Lodged gently under my skin years ago.

Search 83

Of her weeping at sunrise
Are many possibilities:
= A demon has shut her up in the loo
To make her miss the dawn prayers.
= She is regretful of not sleeping in my arms.
= The wisdom tooth pain has hit and
forced its way out through the gum.
= She is forced to admit the gravity
And reconciling with foolish Newton.
= She has left her long neck for four men,
So they infected her with bacteria after fumbling with it.
= She has no enough money
To buy a new toupee
For the New Year fancy party.
= She has fired the mercy bullet
At her love no 3.
= She has fallen foul with the rainbow,
So lightning has bitten her ears.

For my weeping at the same time
Is one interpretation:
All the previous possibilities
(Of Nirmana's weeping)
Are wrong.

Search 84

Who are more loyal:
The mourners who attended my funeral procession,
Or those who were absent
Or the pretext of being unable to bear the moving scene?

Nirva was neither absent
Nor present.
She had another slow procession
Walking in my narrow veins.
Despite this,
All the earth's peoples walked in her procession.

On the next day,
News agencies asserted
That Nirva is still alive and I am still alive,
But the mourners have choked inside my veins.

Search 85

The tea-cup was happy
When by chance fell into it
Twenty beautiful butterflies.
It wished to be targeted by a black fly
To willingly die there.

I was incomparably delighted
When Nirmana trained her aerial kiss precisely
On my tongue,
And responded to my wish of the video chat with her
Wearing a new gown in front of the cam.

All the keys to the universe were in my hand for 70 nights
Until Nirmana told me that
Her torrential aerial kisses
Had shot down seven civilian planes out of ecstasy
Plus a helicopter carrying troopers,
And that her new gown
Had achieved best views and voting rates
In night programs and contests.
Only then did I congratulate Nirmana using the title "Women of
Ages"
And threw the rusty keys quietly
Into the bed of the sleeping lake.

Search 86

On the Anti-Suicide International Day (September 10th)
I completely refrained from thinking of Nirvana.

Twenty-four hours later,
The doctor told me
My brain was suffering from malnutrition.

Search 87

Chocolate Narimana loaded with nuts and desire ...
Her delicious laughs like the coconut heart ...
Her tears are sweeter than rose water ...
Her highway ... Narrow streets ...
Her turns ... squares ... cabarets ... tunnels
Her gums do not perish by chewing ..
Vigilance which is rife even in the few hours of sleep ..,
... All allied to fetch me out of the fridge.

Did not I raise my hand to hold the hook
Coming from the caring sky.
I am well aware that
The meat stored at room temperature spoil
Or when exposed to gold sunlight
Even if it is not permissible to slaughter in violation of "Sharia"

I had also no earnest desire
To be put in the presto pan
Before the grandchildren feel really hungry.

Search 88

Nirmana's major sin
Is that she sees my sin clearly.

My major sin
Is that I do not I have any sin.

Search 89

Do I fear for my fragile toy to break
Like any child playing?
Or I fear my break
Like a toy in the hands of a crazy child?

Tita,
Who of us is the toy.. and who the threads?
Who the threads. who is the finger?
Who the engine.. who the energy?
Who I... Who you?

Search 90

My body has received the whooping cough well
And dental caries
Fungi of the feet,
Because I have secured
Three prescriptions in one go:
They are enough to prove I am alive
Before the jury.

After midnight
I whispered to the doctor in his ear:
"Whenever I feel like I have recovered from Nirmana,
I hate medicine
And long for a very active disease. "

Search 91

Yesterday,
I steeled to play with my wife packs.
We rowed on the table 52 cards and two Jokers
No card is like Nirmitta's face;
The backs of the cards, repeated, are similar to my back.

After each one of us arranged the rows of cards in front of him
And is ready to play,
Suddenly emerged playful Nirmitta.
She pulled all the cards very lightly
To spur and disarrange them in record time.

When we intended to play again,
We did not find the cards.
However, we found Nirmitta has turned into a trampoline.
Then, we were able to play together above.

Search 92

Is Nirma's multi-hued speech really
Free of dyes, artificial condiments
Additional sugar, and preservatives?

Is my speech really
Colourless, tasteless and without smell?

Search 93

Naked girls
In optical mobile advertisements
Blowed at City's crowded cars
Kisses machine coated
And distributed the price lists of goods on passers
With fingerprint-free, full-fat palms.

When official sources said:
"Norita worked as an ads girl "
I ascertained on the spot
That the sole advertisement she designed and played a starring part
Is the her own advertisement
The moment of her great launch
To liberate the land of advertisement.

Search 94

The Earth Images of the outer space claim
That the Nona came from Pluto.

The Pluto Images of the earth claim
The Nona has broken the living egg
She had stolen from my dead neighbors
And coloured it with my vivid brush
On the Spring Day.

Search 95

Whenever I invite Nirmana to my table,
She leaves me to go to her guests.

Whenever I decide to leave her to the guests,
She leaves to ask me for my guests.

Which concerns me much
Is a bowl of soup
Who wishes us to drink it together
So as not to cool off ever.

Search 96

I + Nirma = I
(Although certainly Nirma ≠ zero)

I - Nirma = zero
(With the "I" ≠ certainly Nirma)

I × Nirma = I÷ Nirma
(With the Nirma certainly ≠ ± 1)

Traditional mathematics
Needs to be reconsidered
After the emergence of special laws of Nirma
To estimate the relative and absolute values.

Search 97

Thick steam,
Which went out of the bottle
Appeared at first glance like a huge Effret.

Not scary at all
Perhaps because it reminded me of the bright future
(At a distance of seven light-years from the zero hour)
When I come out of the magic lantern,
Laughing women and children
With gifts for all,
Even for Santa Claus himself.

The gift I will send to Norena in "DHL"
To her secret mailbox
(Above the surface of the moon)
Is a very sophisticated mobile
In order to be able to receive my new music
Through the Bluetooth.

I also send to her my hemispheres
To polish it with Glance
So they look like transparent crystals.
I will ask her as well (as a matter of excess tantalization)
To sprinkle me with itching powder through the air
where the weather forced me to shower
Sulfur soap and water

Search 98

On the escalator
She slowly went up
Without losing any calories.

On the stairs
Landed Nirmana
Quickly like a rock falling from the mountain top.

After 12 months of my climbing and her landing
I reached up to a white cloud in the clear sky;
Nirmana and went to the same cloud.

Strangely, Nirmana asked me when we first met
To land on my escalator
After its reverse operation.

I agreed to immediately
Requiring to allow me to step up
Over the steps of the stairs.

Search 99

Brown clay,
Which was heated in my hands
War missiles have frozen it.
Psychological warfare that was practiced against me violently
With all having known I am a skilful cook,
Able to use expired food
Without anyone knowing.

I wish to maintain trade secrets
To be able to fry the last rib of Nirma
In hydrogenated oil
And distribute to the hungry people lining up in front of mosques
As a person, respected and reputable.

The only consolation,
Which warmed the cockles of my heart
Was that the one who broadcast to the public that I am a false coin
Is the same whom humans predatory animals are aware
That her raw ribs
Are not subject to the Food Standards
According to 2007 AD.

Search 100

The tent which hosted Nirma,
After landing from the exploding comet,
Is hauled by ropes of dead languages.

Pickets to prevent flight in the air
Like any hollow tent
Are like my spiked bones,
Which are not affected by factors such as erosion.

Land that was stuck by the pickets with warmth and greed
Is a literal translation of what is uttered by Nirma
For thousands of years
And never does.

Search 101

Nirma told me
She fears tricky questions
About the strawberry spot, which hit her white dress
In an embarrassing area,
And it is for this reason (very negligible, from my point of view)
She decided to withdraw from all my ribs
For fear that my heart would be a grain of strawberry.

Jokingly I said to her:
"I am not the scandal, of course,
The scandal is your acute view
Through which you thought you've cut the neck of the scandal "

Search 102

Nirma asked me about the common rituals of love
In my dusty planet, which declared bankrupt
I said to her:
"Taxes are a very special
Meticulously calculated one
As it must be accompanied by a kiss 25
For each hour spent in bed other than her bed."

She told me tone like dust, air, water and fire
From within her bedfrill
After she made a hole as wide as
The size of the rupture of her embarrassment and mine:
"You kiss me, then, 750,
Your mature sum of my flaming emotions
Over 30 days"

Search 103

There was no need
To the drums and horns
For the invading forces to declare war
On my peaceful town
Which is still rich in precious stones
And diverse sources of energy
And hearts that know no rust.

The justifications for the military campaign are very flimsy.
Least laughable are:
The desire to trim the fingernails of men .. All men
In the areas of my peaceful town
To become more tender when caressing their women
In order not to scratch themselves with unclean water and cheap
cologne when taking a shower every morning.

Details of the crime are very tragic
Least mean are:
Hundreds of children to dissolve in sulfuric acid,
Then apologizing politely
For these technical errors and laboratory
(Unintentional of course!)

Everyone around me went away
Fearing the repeated massacres;
Apartment Furniture t escaped fugitive,
Clothing,
And footwear.

My bulging pillow refused to abandon me;
It stuck to my bare breast like a stray bat
Perhaps because it does not have an alternative solution
Or because it wants to assume a heroic feat
In the last moments of its life.

I do not know why I questioned it
And decided to know the real reason for its bulge:
Did it inject itself with overdoses
Of the light of late violet lamp?
Or is it filled with gunpowder,

With the aim of the bombing itself, and blowing me at any
moment?

This latter
Made me fear pricking it with a knife,
And the knife, in fact, is no longer with me!

I learned from the Internet,
Which is still high-speed
In free-service access points
Near the public toilets,
That Nirma topped the list of countries receiving refugees
Of all nationalities without exception.

Never did I imagine myself as a political refugee.
I hate politics too much.
I hate the very idea of asylum.
In adolescence, I never had the right to emotional asylum
To any female.
Perhaps after assassinating me and martyrdom,
I request the right of asylum to history
To prove that my blood stored in the refrigerator
Always is fit for planting
In the veins of the areas of peaceful town,
And that my DNA forever carries
The genome of the unpeaceful men.

I read as well as in web pages
In many dialects understood by the majority party
About friendly fire,
Hunting deceived humans
As the flame of the candle hunts butterflies.

Which made me optimistic
By three inches
And stick to my right to legal breathing
Under the guise of fumes.
I was able to conclude a deal online
For the purchase of a set of missiles
Internationally prohibited
Maybe to use them to eliminate the armies of ants in my limbs
And to disperse the armies in my immune systems
To unfurl the white flag satisfied;

Perhaps I can shed these missiles
From the top of the mountain over
Camps of the coalition soldiers
To play its role effectively
In the destruction of the human brains.

Faint flashes of optimism
Put off by these questions:
• What if one of Nirmanian shrapnel hit my head by error?
• Am I able to continue resistance with a devastated brain?
• Will the invaders withdraw from my town, with the destruction of
their minds by missiles?
• If they are already crazy, why would destroy the Nirmanian
missiles?

Search 104

What is the secret behind Nirmana's anger
When I removed my breast's yellow grass
With an automatic plow?

What is the secret of her happiness
When planted my possessed windpipe
In her manually ploughed soil?

Search 105

Microscope, which has given careful consideration into
One of Nirma's cells
Was not able to read histologically
And was suddenly dizzy.

The living cell told me after that
It blows its own trumpet fluently
To those who viewed it with the naked eye.

as soon as I took off my medical glasses
Started "Nirmzad" the okayed talk
And then
The same sudden dizziness seized me
Before "Nirmzad" entered upon the morn.

Search 106

In the recent tombola,
Which was held on the anniversary of liberation from colonialism,
I did not get any prize
In spite of deiging to pay a hefty bribe
To those on the drawing
And my collecting of over 1000 voting cards
To maximize my chance of winning a valuable prize.

The ceremony officials
Told me that a high-ranking security authority
Intervened at the last moment
To prevent any my winning of any prize
After the leak of the news of
"Nirmana's occupation of my central nervous system".

The feeling of injustice is to kill me;
They are all celebrating the liberation.
The ceremony officials
.. And the security men,
Sold their central and non-central nervous systems
To foreign bodies
A long time ago, and cashed the price
Therefore Nirmana did not find a good ground other than me
To be occupied without resistance, and free of charge.

The only condition,
Which was approved by Nirmana
Before gently her colonization of me...,
Is to undertake to stay for as long as possible
For me to guarantee that my good soil turns into a sky.

Search 107

To avoid the potential risk,
Nirmana perforce agreed-- before it is too late--
To the installation of high-quality regulator valve into her spout
For the insatiable butane oven
To take of her effortlessly gushing gas
More than its fair share,
Necessary to ignite the six eyes
And the deeply hidden oven.

I realized too late
That the splendid explosion I had been looking for
Requires unplugging the regulator valve from my organ
And not only set my beloved's eyes
And the hidden oven to fire.

Search 108

Like any professional thief
Used to climbing ropes
And breaking in luxury residential units,
I nimbly moved up the musical keys
Wearing a "safety glove,"
Which Nirmita had spun for me
Or toyed with me for its sake,
In a pioneering attempt by me
To steal a precious ingenious lyric
From the head of a famous composer
Or catching the singing birds of rare species
To immure it in my rib cage
Or plant some of its precious segments
In my hoarse pharynx.

After several steps on the regular stairs
"Ni," ... "Ri" ... "Me" ... "Ta"
I found a large jewelry box
Inlaid with scales.
Its narrow holes pointed out
That the inside is exactly what I hope
My heart danced joyously
To the rhythm of the amazing surprise.

Despite this remarkable success,
My poineering attempts ended in failure
The thousand keys I held failed
To open the box:
It was necessary
That Nirmita should have granted me from the beginning
"The sool key ".

Search 109

At the next Olympic,
Maybe I'll have a gold medal
In the game of love
After I have been well-trained
To overcome all the runners in the marathon
To embrace the kind Nirmana first.

It is not really good
To stand smiling on the tripartite podium
Among two other leopards
I know that they were able to embrace her before.

If I were to re-draft the competition regulations,
I would recommended to eat, rather than embrace, Nirmana
To guarantee that no leopard could find any of her bones
afterwards.

Search 110

When she crossed the old marble bridge
From the Freedom Square to the Wax Museum,
Nirmana decided as usual
To fully respect traffic signals.

Once the sign "The maximum load million people",
I immediately exempted her from the pitfalls of embarrassment
As I soon rid my densely populated self
For Nirmana to pass safely
Carrying on board hundreds of thousands
Of loyal non-rioters
Ready for display to the visitors to the museum.

Search 111

After the Nirvana pressed the key "Delete"
To erase my name from the list of those whom she awakens every
morning,
I became unable to wake up in the morning.
(Nirvana now - as I imagine --
awakens the same morning every morning.)

After Nirvana stopped singing every evening,
I became unable to wake up in the evening.
(Nirvana now - as I imagine --
warbles to awaken the evening every evening.)

After Nirvana leave behind the clouds,
She will - as I imagine – lapse into a coma day and night,
And perhaps I revive my consciousness.

Search 112

Throughout the day of the Minor Bairam,
No one can prolong their life Nirvana's saliva
According to the uncanny prescriptions
In alternative medicine books.

The only being
Which increased by 72 hours old
Is the month of fasting.

Search 113

On the Orphan's Day,
I wished I replaced the the cunning fetus
Carefully hidden in the abdomen Nirmana
Not to be drawn by the time magnet
In order for no one to realize
That it is the shrewd demon,
That fires rockets in the spaces
Either to play
Or to positively protest against
The nature through humans.

Is it really true Nirmana is responsible for nursing the negative crescents
To become full-fledged moons?
Do full moons really erode after their arbitrary weaning
To sink into the Sea of Forgetfulness?

Search 114

"The small dolphin
did not Want anything from the naughty girl
But to save her
from the stormy waves of the sea
Contaminated with human waste,
Injected with submarines' guiles and malignant waste.

"Upon their arrival to the life beach
Which was crowded with sticky lichen and smooth rocks,
The girl joyfully left the dolphin's back.
She granted it seven rainow-coloured balloons,
A red popsicle colored with desire
Where an innocent smile had been drawn on her face,
Saying "Bye" gently and politely.
Her eyes glittered with no tears.

"The dolphin then did not think of
Taking private lessons in selfishness
And turning gradually
From a bulging rubber life buoy
Into a giant island
Capable of accommodating sea mares
Which lose their balance in the water. "

I, too, did not know
Why I decided to tell the story to Tita
Although she is neither protected against the loss of balance
In the sea, land and air
Nor am I never a dolphin!

Search 115

The idols worshipped by pagans
The righteous strongly destroyed
And rubbed them in the sand.

Is that which prevented me from sculpting the statue of Nona
My fear that somebody might worship it
Or that somebody might destroy it?

Search 116

I do not need my organs
Therefore I announced in the press
My desire to donate all of them.

Surprisingly, I discovered that it is not required from anyone,
Or perhaps no one reads newspapers well.

Nirvana need all her organs.
I also need all her organs,
Therefore I announced in the press
That her organs are registered in her name,
And there is no desire of their conveyancing.

Surprisingly, I discovered
That Nirvana did not have appendix
To get rid of it one day,
Nor does she ever cut her hair with scissors
Or clips her nails with a nail-clipper.

Search 117

All humans have realized
That Nirmana is a nature reserve,
Where it is not allowed to touch her rare flora and fauna
And a military exclusion zone.

Alone, I grabbed a rifle,
And began chasing white pigeons in their skies.
Whenever a shot was fired,
A feather –like a projectile-- befell my head.

The banquet I tantalized my hungry soul with
Turned in front of my eyes to a massacre.
I'm all its victims.
Then the pigeons alighted in the evening
To pick my remains with their beaks.

Search 118

Only three tablets from the natural medicine "Nirmalin"
Were more than enough
To find 3 years of my nightmarish life had passed safely
Without knowing anything about them.

Despite the many possibilities,
What is 100% certain is that
These tablets had never been sleeping tablets.

Search 119

For my desire to stick fully to Nirmana,
I did not stop at divesting myself of my clothes,
But I also got rid of my whole skin.

Nirmana did not expand, nor shrink,
When I saw the burning ball of meat
Moving to her nets
But she was skillfully able to
Build a wall between us.
She lined all the rocks,
Except for a stone not in place.

To date, Nirmana did not tell me
Which one of the means of execution she prefers:
To just peep at her from
The narrow hole in the wall,
Or I place the last stone with my hand
To complete the separation wall between us,
And each one of us is totally relieved of the other?

Search 120

Difficultly enough,
I was able to paint a picture
Similar to Nirmana's features
The moment I saw her on the earth.

I made it the wallpaper
To my personal computer's screen.

Every morning, I boot the machine
So the features of the image grow by a day.

Ten years later,
The features will certainly
By 10 years.

Half a century later,
Perhaps the picture dies
While Nirmana remains forever
Retaining her features
I saw the moment she appeared on the earth.

Search 121

Under the old tree
In the park for pets and wild animals,
I lay a dead beat,
A day after a warm dry
Without air and smiles.

Always in my bag, there is a moisturizing cream for the skin.
I did not use it that night
For I felt sense my soul is suffering from cracks.

With my nails I dug a large hole next to the tree
To bury two pieces of my backbone
And two handfuls of my youth memories
And middle-age dreams.

I was shocked by such a large number of insatiable worms.
The intertwined roots of the tree forced me to respect them.

I wished at that moment two things:
= My lymphocytes and Nirvana's glands intertwine on the face of
the erath and below.
= The melting of a piece of Nirvana's glands like a piece of butter
   To heal with it the cracks in my soul.

Search 122

The poor who speculate on the Stock Exchange
Do not realize that they are all losers
For Nirva
Decided to dynamite all economic transactions
And abolish all ancient coins
For her to be the only
Precious paper in circulation among humans.
Either they understand well its value
Or understand well that
They have no value without it.

Search 123

A bright hair in my tail
Makes me turn back too much.

One night
I asked Noritta to put it out
So as not to collide with someone or something during my typical
walk.

Noritta refused to convert to inert gas
Or a bottle of water.

What I considered "cold shower" indeed
Is that Noritta that ignited the four main directions
And all sub ones.

I fully stopped the mechanical movement
To dedicate myself to the control of my tail,
And study the latest news ignitions around me
Very thoroughly
Worthy of pantheons of geography
And the kings of off-tracts.

Search 124

She said to me Nirmana:
"You cannot erase the woman except by a woman."

I said to her:
"That is true;
  It is also true that I can erase you with my tongue."

She said to me:
"That is true;
  It is also true that you have no tongue."

Search 125

The simple farmers have not given up
Inspection with their small axes
For the debris of a wondrous, marble cloud
Said to have suddenly fallen from the seventh heaven
Not in the form of rain carrying blessings and dust,
Nor in the form of shrapnel raging like volcanic lava.

Alone,
I arrived at an astonishing interpretation of the disappearance of the
cloud:
Nirvana has picked up its debris
From the seventh land
And gave it - secretly - to seventh sky
On its birthday.

Search 126

"The breakfast invitation
Nirma sent to the address of my house
Sealed with a rosy kiss
I accepted warmly
Although I was not used to start my day with breakfast.

"The delicious hot lunch
Which she fed me with her hands in my mouth
(I swear to God, "with her hands in my mouth"!)
Lured me into undergoing frequent surgical operations
To expand my stomach.

"The dinner, which I excelled in preparing for Nirma
- after I had become unable to taste life without her --
She apologized for not coming to it in offensive language.
She simply said she always eats alone!
(I swear to God, she said it so simply.)

In the morning
I steeled to fire the mercy killing bullet at myself
In agreement with my private doctor
(Who is very good and sincere)
But Nirma had another view,
Where she was able to convince the doctor
(Who is very good and sincere)
That slow death is the most appropriate solution
For a bore, like me,
Who loves chewing memories to the last breath."

I was very astonished I had recorded that guff in my diary
Although I am well aware
That Nirma had never let me breakfast with her
And never fed me in my mouth with her hands;
Never did I invite her to dinner with me.
My private doctor
Is also not good and sincere to that extent!

Search 127

When delicious Mitta put on her precious stones,
And dropped a non-precious stone in the stagnant lake,
I felt temporarily sick.
I wistfully asked:
"Am I the projectile or the projectile in it?"

Search 128

With the horse's cut tail,
I failed to shoo away the swarms of flies
Stuck to my thighs.

I thanked Nirmana very much
When she handed me a flexible plastic swatter
Which can kill more than one a fly in one smack.

Quite amazingly,
The swatter pained me much
When smacking my dead thighs repeatedly
While a single fly did not die.

Most surprisingly,
When I hit the thigh of Nirmana onetime
- As a matter of reproach --
The smack pained my own thigh
More than any other strike
And at the same time
Killed all the flies

Search 129

Hysteria which seized me
When Nirmana approached me
Has no drug than her coming closer to me.

My skin color which has suddenly changed
From black to white
After the partial emergence of Nirmana
Will be completely colorless
After her looming clearer.

Nirmana's active virus
Which has bugged the "operating system"
In all my electronic toolkit
Has little hope of being destroyed
Except through being infected with other Nirmanian viruses.

Search 130

I do not claim to get rid of all my rubbish
By bathing in hot water and soap,
But after each shower,
I feel that my soul is lighter
And that my fingers have no prints.

I do not ever leave the place
Before wiping the condensate water vapor over the shaving mirror.
When I look at the mirror,
I find Nirmana's face most lean
Smiling to me meaningfully.

Search 131

In the last night of the dirty war
The aerial bombardment started calmly
And then rose suddenly.
All the neighbors
In our busy street
Fled to the collective trenches
Once listening to the siren.

I quickly turned off the house lights.
I slipped on my own from the back stairs
Heading to a solitary trench
Nirmana had built specifically for me
While of the Barbarian invaders' backs were turned.

Hours passed peacefully,
Through which I felt that I am a bird in the freedom cage.
I did not know exactly what happened after that,
But most certainly,
The smart missile
Broke through the trench from a ventilation shaft,
And transformed me to a red spot on the wall of resistance
Though a small tear projectile
- Or rather a saliva projectile --
Was enough
To drown me in the deep sea,
Extremely brutal and saline.

Search 132

The hungry will foment a sure revolution
When I swallow Nirmana,
And nothing is left of her.

The lions will foment a sure revolution
When Nirmana swallows me
And nothing is left of me.

Search 133

On the back of one steed,
Which I deemed a thoroughbred
(A group of close friends and I)
I bet in the race, and so did my friends
Without telling anyone.

Narimana bet for herself
Without telling anybody she is able to dress up
And make everyone think she is a horse.

Narimana covered the track distance in record time
While the horse (a group of close friends and I bet for)
fell down
At the first dangerous turn
Admitting that it personally had bet on Narimana
Without telling anyone that it is able to dress up
And make everyone think it is a human being.

Search 134

During the presentation of the first horror series
On the encrypted TV channel "Earth"
Nirma screamed.

During the presentation of the tenth episode
I screamed.

After the presentation of the last episode
All people vanished
And Nirma and I remained alone on the surface of the Earth
For a new unencrypted horror series to start,
Which the earth will not stand even one episode of.

Search 135

I am not allowed to eat legumes (all)
So as not to be defeated by fava anemia
And anemia.

I am not allowed Nona (alone)
So as not to be killed by love anemia
Haemorrhage.

Search 136

I gently said to Nona:
"I plant me a cenotaph
So I visit after my absence."

Plant for yourself a cenotaph
So I, too, visit
After my absence
And yours
And the absence of my cenotaph."

Nona answered violently:
"Plant you your pointed vertical silence
In my flat fertile delta
Full of green words."

Search 137

Unusual
For an extraordinary man like me to stand
In a long queue
In front of the bread outlet.

I stood in line for more than two hours.
When I got to the seller,
I gave him special container in which I locked Nirmana
(Once she came out of the new microwave in my house.)

Enthusiastically I told him:
"Give each and every one of the people (for free)
This soft, appetizing
Loaf always renewable."

Search 138

Days have imbued me with their double standards,
But found me sticking to writing with a quill,
And insisted on refusing to get married to a foreign woman
(with thhe purpose of protecting social cohesion).

At the same time,
I signed the "GATT" agreement with an imported pen
And agreed to become a member of the multinational company
Which caused the collapse of entire communities.

Noon tempted me to cooperate with her
To create limited liability "Noona".
I said to her:
"I am more to be an over -letter
At the end of your trade mark. "

Search 139

Doctors advised the illusion treatment
To eliminate the pain of 30% of patients.

In my cases,
The illusion treatment will not pay
To cure me of Nirma:
She is simply the real pain
Which made the doctors confirm
I - alone – am 70% of patients!

Search 140

"God is great!"
I say it every major bairam,
And begin the slaughter of the same ewe.

"Every year you are the same."
Nirmana always says that in the New Year,
And begins to remove the coating layer of my skin and nails,
Not with the hazardous organic solvent "acetone".

Search 141

Nitta said to me,
Before sleeping in my tent one night:
"I'm your temporary guest, so treat me well."

Oh, poor!
She does not know I am her permanent guest,
Who has no water except her vapour water.

Search 142

Agronomists and meteorologists emphasize
That Nerva is summer fruit.

I bear witness
She has ornamented my home greenhouse
With her cheerful colors
In astringent winter.

Search 143

To accept to be the victory horse Nirma's conquests
Has tempted to request my transformation into a chess piece.
(King is not among them!)

If I approved that,
I would tempt Nirma to transform me into a chess board
With sixty-four squares,
Where pawns flow above, panting,
For fear of death
And in the hope of being preferred.

Search 144

Nirma told me
She had known as many men as her countless hair.
Since I am completely bald,
I told her that I had known as many women as
The countless hair of the men she had known!

She told me that she fully got me
After her long experience,
For I am a man.

I told her I did not get her,
Despite my long experience,
For she is not a woman.

Search 145

Nirmana warmly shook hands with me
After giving a lecture on the "new world order".

Spontaneously she asked me:
"Why do you retain your full palm till now,
While your entire wealth is in one of your finger joints? "

I replied without prevarication:
"I know exactly the area of wealth in the right ring finger,
But I prefer to keep all the poverty lines
In my good palms,
To distribute them to the aspirants rallying around me,
Who think
They - and only they- are the protectors of social justice."

Search 146

The usual leaves,
The casual and sick leaves,
And multiple public holidays,
All do not mean anything to me.

On all days of the year without exception,
I do my hard real job:
I record to attendance signature every morning
In the books of Mrs. Noon
And never leave in the evening.

Search 147

Nirmana asked me about my head capital.
I said to her: "You are my head capital."

I asked her about her head capital.
She said: "My capital has no head."

Search 148

By electing me Chairman of the Muftis,
Nirma is safe from the sword
Despite admitting my murder
And the presence of witnesses - including myself - on the
availability of the intention premeditation.

Search 149

My heart,
Involving the Nirmana,
Wishes to be my skin
To die as soon as he is exposed to what he cannot stand,
Then grows a new heart.

I wish
 Nirmana renews her cloak
Once
For me to rest
Once
From the hassle of renewing what I wear.

Search 150

The Nirmana's face appeared
On the optical billboard
In the heart of the city.
Is it the evidence for defusing consumer durables,
Or evidence that Nirmana
Is the new phosphorous army
Capable of invading human needs?

The appearance of my dimmed face
Near the optical billboard
Is the conclusive evidence
I am the two-times losing army
- In the battle for access to consumer goods
- And in the battle of getting
An uncooked piece of Nirmana.

Search 151

I usually attend pageants
To make sure that he whom I am looking is absent.

I attend the fashion shows
To ensure that full nudity is still the best.

I attend wrestling rounds
To make sure I am the pain human beings cannot tolerate.

I attend family events
To ensure that there are days
With the taste of the four seasons.

I attend the ceremonies of Nirma's signing of her new books
To make sure I am her very old book!

Search 152

The distance between the white thread
And the black one
Is fully equivalent to the distance between my right eye
(Which is aware of the distance
Between the white and black threads)
And my left eye
(Which are not aware of the distance
Between the white and black threads).

How did Nirmana not realize the distance between me and myself?
How did I not realize
The distance between me and myself?

Search 153

Before time is completely eroded
By rust
I cut it with a chainsaw
At the middle line:
Half for Nirmana at my own will
And half for her…at her own will.

I,
My name has become "The Bitten"…forever
At the will of the wall clock,
Which has derived its rhythm from the regular pace my heart beats.

The question moves in my throat
Anti-clockwise is:
"How does the human being remain in place,
Then is banished outside time?"

Search 154

Since it is impossible to "secure" an alternative,
The official governor did not approve giving a very short leave to
Nirmana
To rest from the actual governance.

Search 155

By dealing the dice six million times,
Each number appeared about a million times,
And Nirmana appeared six million times
Because she is - simply - all the natural numbers
(And the unnatural too),
Except for "zero",
Who am I without her.

Search 156

The rumour that had it I would be sold in subsidized form
Did not draw the attention of Nirmana:
She is not worthy of subsidies like the mob
Nor am I a popular commodity to that extent.

Search 157

All life insurance companies
Refused to deal with me
To prove I am not at all normal.

The password is, of course, Noona.
The difference between the one hypnotically doped like me
And the one clinically doped at hospitals
Is that their suffering ends with the triumph of medicine over illness
While my suffering will end
With medicine completely surrendering to illness
And raising the white flag (my deferred shroud).

Search 158

Exposure to shake the nets five times
At one go
Did not urge me to criticize goalkeepers.
All the blame I fastened to the nets themselves,
Which shook stupidly honestly
With each shot of Nirma

Search 159

Fear of my extinction
- Where there is no wedge but me --
Urged me to marry a hare.

It was easy for me to repeatedly delve into her
- In the "box" and not in the lab --
And yelp dozens of people in one year
Out of five births or more
Since the uterus regains its composure
After six hours of birth.

The fear of Nirmana's extinction
- Where there is no way
    To remove pickets from conception but she --
Urged me to get a PhD in genetic engineering
In the hope of cloning her in my laboratory.
I was much encouraged to this,
For I am skilled in authoring science fiction
for super children,
Who do not resemble rabbits.

Search 160

In the last presidential elections,
I was keen to go early
To the polls.

And marked "True" next to "Chaos",
Who is a candidate worthy of respect
Not only because it resembles Nirmana,
But also as the fittest for the leadership of our torn country.

Search 161

I to the drum:
"I beat you regularly;
  The result is art."

Nirma to me:
"I beat you irregularly;
  The result is also art."

I to myself:
"There are, therefore, methods of calculation
- The settling of scores --
  More creative than the multiplication table."

Search 162

The heavy rain in the street did not distract
Me from my beloved who was walking with me
Under one umbrella.

Successive television images
Sprayed by a satellite TV dish
Directly over my head
Fully immersed me in the isolation sea.

In my isolation, I did not watch out for the telephone ring,
Which courted me several times,
Which angered my beloved;
She refused to go with me on the street the next day
Under one umbrella.

I did also not feel as the terrorist who broke into the apartment
And hid in the wardrobe a bomb
That can be detonated by remote control.

I did not note that the picture of Nirmana in my coat pocket
Had been covered in fire water,
And caused serious damage to it.

Search 163

The reason is unknown,
The reason for the concept of the extreme interest
On the part of the reactionaries
In achieving "cultural cross-fertilization"
between the fine thread and the narrow eye of the needle,
Though sewing has become a threadbare profession
In the next stage, at least,
Where people steeled to a long stand
In the column of the de-skinning,
And Nirmana and I steeled
To enter the cell of nudity and torture together,
Charged with column dissent.

Search 164

One puff of unknown origin in 35 candles
Was sufficient to blow it all
And to ignite a new year of my life
Which will explode without mutely exactly 12 months later
Dividing the cake into as many pieces
As the number of attendees,
Who will they know me, and I not.

I wish Nirmana attends with them,
To tell me they are my family and loyal friends
To confirm to me that I simply the owner of the miraculous puffer
Which extinguished the candles,
And triggered the exploding year.

Search 165

I bounced into the wall strongly.
Nirmana said gasping:
"I feel for you;
The following bounce will be to your enemy, God willing."

Her prayers seem to be quickly answered,
For I bounced into the wall once again.

Search 166

In virtual worlds
Thousands of young people and adults are involved in clashes (N-Game).
The result means nothing to no one;
Happiness is the candy eaten by everyone
With the strokes on the keyboard.

Alone,
In the real world of great bitterness,
Ninja men chase me,
Robots,
And the supernatural powers
All allied against my head, and the result means much to them.
They beat me a thousand times per day
These are the encounters (N-Game) in the revised version
Which Ms. "N" indulged me with.

Search 167

A red signal from my eyes
Promised me danger,
So I did not cross the mirror.

A red signal from her cherry-like mouth
Tempted me to cross.

Nirma:
"Who hit me?
Is your tongue faster than sound?! "

Search 168

I have prepared well
With pre-hunger,
Against the siege imposed on my country
(Like other hot targets).
I have prepared well
With serious medical procedures
(Not worthy of a skinny man like me),
Such as reducing the size of the stomach and intestine overcome.

The siege imposed by Nirma
To my territorial waters
Cannot be prepared for with special training loads
(With the exception of clinical death).

Search 169

Since I believe that Nirmana will be the universe singer,
I was on writing a lyric and composing music for her.

When Nirmana heard it,
She did not like it
Not only because it is in English,
Which does duly not show the merits of her voice
But also because she did not like the wordings.

Nirmana advised me to write in another language
And change the words from
"I am informed that all times are bad"
To
"We have to forget all times ...
  The best time ... is the human being."

I did like the opening,
But not being proficient in any other language (not English)
Precluded the completion of the song,
Thus I temporarily waived
The dream of fame and wealth.

Search 170

Despite the defeat of myself
I collected 15 points
Winning in five games
In the Six Continents Champions League.

Nirmana is outside the official competition;
Nevertheless,
She collected 21 full points
Winning over six competitors,
And excelling over herself.

Search 171

While I am in the coffin embalmed
And the mourners around me writing their obits in secret ink
On plain farewell handkerchiefs,
Narimana whispered in my ear:
"Speak and smile or I will be angry with you!"
Upon this, the wooden coffin developed a tongue
And thus its face became ☺.
I
Was able to speak
only four words in front of everyone:
"I'm not really here"

Search 172

Physicist Ohm
Simply proved to me
I was the shortest man in the universe,
For the human resistance power connector of Nirvana
Is in converse relation with its length.
I have no appreciable resistance.

Search 173

An elderly woman selling bread
Requested to see me urgently
At the headquarters of public voluntary work.

I steeled to hear problem related to her,
But I was surprised that the problem is related to her miserable
bread,
As it was suddenly infected with loss of appetite,
And it was no longer capable of fragmentation in the mouths of the
hungry
After Nirmana had claimed the title of "Lady of the Table"
In the last Giants Championship
Held in the largest orphanages in the Middle East.

I advised the old woman
To apologize to her bread
And assist it in the disposal of its identity
As a commodity bought and sold
In order to win more cups and titles.

Search 174

The shortest message in history
Was one from my mobile to Nirmitta's mobile.
I wrote to her: (?!)
Surprisingly, she was surprised at unjustified prolongation,
And asked me to look for: (.)
To stop the flood of my violations.

Search 175

At the beginning of each month,
I donate a bottle of blood
To the "Red Crescent".

At the beginning of each year,
I sell a plot of land from my property
To finance my long journey
To search for Nirmana's picture,
Which fell out of my fist my day
Somewhere.

What I seriously think of now
Is the fate of "Red Crescent" patients
After my blood to loses its ability to regenerate
And my fate
After selling all my land ..
To stand for the last span,
And also sell all my organs
To private hospitals.

Then, I would feel I am a foolish gambler;
Perhaps I hate the image of the lost Nirmana
Because she has not made any real effort
In order to get close to the fists of my hands.

Search 176

The small boat,
Which steeled to escape the flood
Had no room for a couple
From all species of humans, animals and plants.

In a few moments, seats filled;
Only one seat left.

I cynically suggested that
I hide inside Nirmana
Or she hides inside me
To win the seat empty together.

The very tragic end is that
Nirmana preferred to face of the flood without me,
While I refused to board the boat without her,
Not really aware of what happened after that
Nor where am I now.

Search 177

Prior to the legendary bird laid
Its egg called "Planet Earth",
Nirmitta had been an open sky, with a changing weather.
I had been a sparrow flying sky high
With small wings and a tail, and without a beak.

When the sky became a giant glass cage,
Endothermic at a temperature of 37 ° C,
The bird immediately fled
To dive into the layers of the Earth
Searching in the sedimentary rock units
For the Nirmittan excavations
Belonging to one of the geological ages.

Search 178

I apologized to the police officers
After they had searched my apartment and my office and my garage
Searching for Nirmana,
But did not find any trace of her.

They asked me to cooperate with them to arrest her,
And to tell them immediately in the event of her contact with me.

I laughed to my heart and I said to them:
"But I ask that you
To cooperate with me to catch her,
And to tell me immediately if she contacts you!
If Nirmana had violated the terms of your law,
She had planted in my head all the items in her law
A few days before disappearing. "

Search 179

When Nirmana fell by error
In one of the piles of wheat
And was subject to grinding by error
With the poor wheat
In the grinding stone of organisms
Near my house ..,
It was easy for me to pick her up in a few minutes
By sifting tons of flour
With my large-hole sieve of my memory.

When Nirmana melted herself strangely
In the fruit cocktail pack
Placed on my table two months ago,
My memory sieve failed to pick it up
Despite its very narrow holes.

Search 180

Nirma's fresh laughter mixed with
Her very saline tears
In the Personal Status Court.

My heart was mixed with my tongue
When the judge summoned me to hear my confessions
In the divorce case filed by Ms. Nirma.
I said to him:
"Dom ... Dom ... Dom ... Dom ... Dom ... Dom."

Question marks mixed exclamation marks
On the judge's face.
When examining the case file,
He clapped his hands over while eying Nirma.
Then he said quietly
(Quoting the beach judge's wig Abdel Halim Hafez):
"Postpone the case to last January!!
To give the claimant adequate notice
To exclude the official death certificate
Issued in her name a few days ago. "

Search 181

When the truth is stupid,
Man clutches to stupidity
Not to believe it.

So,
When the Nirmana's pieces were distributed
To all nations of the world,
I clutched to the myth of Isis and Osiris.
I am still waiting the day
I collect the scattered parts of my charming one,
And mount her body anew.

Search 182

Are my incisors so sensitive
That they erode
When caressing them with
Toothpaste and brush?

Are my lips so sensitive
That they are liable to cracking
When suddenly attacked
By full-cream kisses
Or rubbing them with cocoa cream?

Is my shadow so sensitive
That it trembles continuously
For fear of treachery stab (it does not deserve)
When I go into a retreat
At my own will,
Preferring to corner away in the dark tunnel?

Are my palms so sensitive
That each one avoids hurting the other
When clapping for Nirmana
When she wiped my tears and infected mucous with her
handkerchief?

Is Nirmana so sensitive
That it has suffered so much a human influenza
And died several times of bird flu
Without having a respiratory system?

Search 183

I do not bless what the ceiling fan is doing,
Perhaps because it revolves in a funny way;
Perhaps for agreeing to remain suspended between heaven and
earth;
Perhaps because it distributes the room air fairly
To those sitting beneath.

Noreena,
Popping out of the roof of the unknown
And diving into the bottom of the unknown
In an unfunny way,
Granted everyone looking at her
100% of her total light
Not detracting from the share anyone.

Search 184

I saw her?
Maybe,
But she did not see me.

I did not see her?
Maybe,
She saw me.

Nirmana,
Sail to the island of negotiations
With my two rising Phoenician pinions.
I will set sail on my sailplane.
A realistic solution may be generated
From this circuit open between us,
That never closes itself.

Search 185

Six checkpoints
I passed all safely
With a national number card in my possession,
And my passport expired.

The seventh and final checkpoint,
Which I reached after Nirmana had been in my possession,
And in which I was exposed to much inhumane interrogations,
And was subjected to hard smacking,
And ended up totally naked
Even of "health"!

To the moment I am searching for Nirmana
Directly under my skin
(Where I had hidden before reaching the checkpoint).
Did she get out with the beads of sweat
When beatings hardened,
Or did it melt in my blood,
So my immune cells swallowed her?!

Search 186

To ignite my traditional feelings of
About my traditional women,
I allotted my entire fossil fuel,
Not heeding its imminent depletion
After a century two.

My clean renewable energy
And my nuclear energy
Are allotted to heat my polar soul
To be able to continue to live
After the provisional disappearance of Nirmana
Or depletion forever.

Search 187

Narimana treaded rock,
So it softened for her.

Narimana treaded water,
So it became rock for her.

Narimana walked barefoot on the mud,
So it was the resurrection of human beings
And hers
While I remained alone in between,
Neither from human beings
Or from Narimana's species.

Search 188

On one dish of scales
I sat before the appearance of Nirmana.

On the other dish
I sat down after her disappearance.

Surprisingly, the two dishes balanced equally,
Which assured me
That all my actual life was
Outside the timeframe.

Search 189

Just as a nation which forgot its immortality,
So did the age forget Nirvana.

Just as a mother who forgot her baby's birth
In the ninth month,
So did Nirvana forget me.

Search 190

I'm not a superpower.
It is not my right to use the veto
To defend my interests and the interests of allies;
But despite this,
I am the owner of the two famous vetoes the history of humankind:
On my date of birth,
I vetoed uniformity by not crying
So much so they thought me dead.
On the day of Nirmana's demise,
I vetoed uniformity by crying
So much so they thought me alive.

Search 191

Formerly, I could not believe my father
When he told me that his manual watch
Operated without a battery
And without any clear source of energy.

Now,
My father does not believe
I am operating without Nirvana.

Search 192

Very painful
Are memories of pigeons
In the small village,
The destination of dozens of fishermen each morning,
From neighboring countries.

Very painful
Are memories of the "Panadol Woman"
With headache man.

Very painful
Are memories of the cocoon
With the silkworm,
Which is always moving.

More painful than my memories with Nirma
Is that they do not have painful memories.

Search 193

Remorse is pressing me hard,
For I never did send any gift to Nirva.

If the wheels of life have to go backwards,
To be more precise:
If I once again flew out of time and space,
I would send Nirva a bunch of flowers
And write on the small card:
"The most beautiful gift,
Which set Santa Claus himself to shame,
Because it is not able to reward anyone with,
Is your visage."

Search 194

Multinational forces failed
To secure the areas of conflict between me and myself
On three small islands
Rich in natural gas
Necessary to ignite an extinguished soul.

The superpower is bent proclaiming one of myself governor
And the other dissident.
Surprisingly, it supports the two parties with arms
(The governor is me before the appearance of Nirmana
The dissident is me after an absence of Nirmana).

Nirmana is not aligned to any of the parties of the conflict,
But she is anxious about the natural gas,
Which will undoubtedly be depleted
As soon as the governor or dissident starts to inhale.

Search 195

Which one is the mirror:
The lake, which reflected the sky,
Or the sky which reflected the lake?
In any case,
I do not need to concave and convex mirrors,
Not even a flat one,
I see my "natural" face
Which sank in grief
After reports of the sinking of Nona
In "abnormal" circumstances.

Yellow sand is a mistranslation of
My sudden bankruptcy disaster.
Snails are a safe purse for my few money
Enough to buy my needs
Of the rock candy
And marshmallows.

With each wave coming from the unknown
I am seized by a mad desire
To putt the rocks
Perhaps my blood spills
And rocks become less adamant
Or perhaps the rock oozes blood,
So I make sure I am harsher than stones.

"Noon" (i.e. 'whale') which swallowed Nona
Will give it back to the beach
On a moonlit night...,
As I saw in my sleep!

I cannot be certain: May I have the right to doubt
- Just doubt --
I have a vision?!

What I am really certain of is:
This dream usually invades me in very warm,
Damp nights,
Where I sleep in a pool,
And also invades me
When I sleep in the rain.

Search 196

More important for the dead machine
Than electricity and the operating system is
To be able to do feel death throes whenever you want.

With the emergence of Nirmana
My language turned from the "one zero"
To "zero and one".
Nevertheless,
You I do not accept to be described as a machine
Perhaps because the most important "instructions" Nirmana,
Which I stick to is:
Not to follow any instructions!

With the disappearance of Nirmana
My language turned to "one one"
Which is, of course, she.

Search 197

Listening to Nirma
Ended in my sheer silence.

Listening to her silence,
Will it end in my abstinence from silence and speech?!

Exposure to the Nirma fountain
Ended in drowning asphyxia over drowning
Will the exposure to the remains of Nirma's perfume,
End in drowning asphyxia in memories?

Search 198

Between the "action" and "reaction"
Nothing but "additive conjunctive",
Which is very peaceful, but even negative.

Between me and myself
Nothing except "N",
Not as "additive conjunctive"
But as an affirmative and negative particle
At the same time!

Search 199

The prints of shoes on the sand
Confirm that the soldiers passed from here
On their way to the border and barbed wire
Perhaps to secure the weapons of the past
And possibly to totally eliminate them with
Weapons of the future.

Sands and atomic fallout of Nirmana
Over the skin and my shoes leather
Assert that she violated the border and the barbed wire,
Passing from somewhere
To somewhere.

Search 200

The final caftan,
Which my beloved one called "wall calendar" took off
Defeated me hugely
As it reminded me of 365 days of failure
On which I tried to hunt naked Nirmana.

(Translated by Amr El-Zawawy)

"The robot in search of a way"
(Interview with the poet Sharif Al-Shafiey, Al-Ahram Weekly Newspaper)

The publication of Sharif Al-Shafiey's new collection of poetry has sent ripples through the Arab world's literary scene. Mohamed Nabil interviews the poet.

The latest work by Egyptian poet Sharif Al-Shafiey is part of a large poetic project entitled The Complete Collection of a Robot. For poetry readers it is a stone thrown into still water, and has been referred to by critics and intellectuals from Egypt and the Arab world as a highly original piece of work with a catchy content and artistic format. The poems represent a great change in recent Arabic poetry.

Since the first part of this project, "Searching for Nirmana with Smart Fingers", was published in Cairo in Arabic it has received dozens of reviews in leading Arab newspapers.

With this collection, his fourth collection of poems, Al-Shafiey, 40, breaks new ground in that it is wholly narrated by a rebellious robot launched into the various paths of life and spheres of the universe with an intrinsic courage and freedom. The robot pays no attention to and even ridicules the radio waves that remotely "control his mechanical movement and path". This is an innovative robot that not only breaks away from the rules of the herd and opposes the laws that turn man into machine, but rebels against the economic, political, military, social and scientific innovations of his age; innovations that have enclosed man within a dark tunnel.

What is it that has motivated the robot to carry out this "artistic assault" on life?

"It is real life itself that has pushed him to attempt to search for it, sense its physics with the fingers and detect the essence of the soul which has not yet completely vanished," says Al-Shafiey, who also works in the media field.

Al-Shafiey is known for his adventures in the world of poetry; he is the author of the longest poem in modern Arabic poetry, entitled: "Colors Tremble Covetously", 1,035 pages.

Al-Shafiey's collections of poems are: "Between the Two of Them, Time Gets Rusty", 1994, "All by Himself, He Listens to the Concerto of Chemistry", 1996, and "Colors Tremble Covetously", 1999.

Also published by Al-Shafiey is a study on the role of place in the works of Naguib Mahfouz, under the title of "The Popular Districts in the Novels of Naguib Mahfouz, between Reality and Innovation", in 2006.

"The contaminated air in his room forced him to open the 'window' improve the ventilation; the 'window' can be a real one overlooking a view and detecting things in a direct way, and it can be jumped from too. It can also be an electronic window used to search electronically for Nirmana and her spectra," he explains.

The robot has decided on unprecedented withdrawal, or, in other words, initiate a risky adventure, the outcome of which cannot be measured. He has decided to withdraw from the mechanised and extensively disciplined universal room that is valid for a mechanically and digitally polluted life with calculated dimensions, but which is still a non-airy room where the soul can find no joy.

Moving from a fake, geometrical life that is parallel in nature to the essence of death, to a hypothetical and chaotic one, the robot can search for his distinct humanity and be free to chase his hypothetical Nirmana with her varied names and forms, in the existence of which he is the only believer.

What justifies this exhausting journey at this particular juncture? According to Al-Shafiey, "Matters have become increasingly cruel in the way man is stripped of his humanity, and in the way his will is effaced and his ability to take decisions is depleted".

"The principle of polarisation has become deeply rooted, while privacy and identity have plummeted to the ground".

"Man, in fact, has become a subjugated machine, while the compelling force is blind machines. The funny thing is that politicians, economists and people of wisdom are concerned about the depletion of the world's energies and are looking for alternative sources of energy, ironically enough, in a world that has basically run out of its spiritual power." He nods his head in agreement with his own words.

So it seems that the innovative robot poet, who has forsaken the submissive and tamed herd, is, in the first place, looking for an energy that is certain to have run out. It is the spiritual energy of his depleted soul that he is looking for, and if he finds it he will later on be able to search for other things.

The end of the book, however, suggests a return to where the robot began.

"In reality, he is back at the point where he has started, without finding either Nirmana or his depleted, 'lost' self. However, he is not back for nothing, since he has already come to realise his individuality and privacy. He has moved against the norms and programmes, and drifted away from the remote control held by a compelling power, and from the supremacy of the discipline; any discipline".

Consequently, Al-Shafiey adds, he has been able to detect the shame of an age fully drowned in materialism, machinery and technology, and has laid his hands on the main economic, political, military, social and scientific innovations that have led humanity to that desperate destiny, where the individual has no place to survive in the midst of the turmoil of smashing the masses, and where all sorts of things -- new births, education, enlightenment, production and consumption and murder -- are based on calculations, even calculations that are excessively arithmetical.

In this sense, the journey can be seen as an end in itself. "That tiring search in itself is of great value and is a call for rebellion and the testing of alternatives, particularly when there is nothing that necessitates caution. I mean, because the kind of life available to us is fake, mummified, and clinically dead and imprisoned in a sterile, universal room, it is therefore quite lovely that Nirmana's sweet virus of rebellion should intrude into such a life".

Nirmana has come from a strange world to lead our robot friend to the unknown; she leads the game from behind the scene. The robot has accepted only the desires of Nirmana because she is the only one who can control him. This is explained in one paragraph: 'Why have I accepted to be easily controlled by Nirmana? Maybe it is because she was enthusiastic about managing me from inside"!

So, is it man or machine that wins in the end?

"For the first part, the battle might seem to have been won by the machine, since the robot here is the hero in some sense. However, it is man, in reality, who is victorious as the robot is simply one who rebels against the rules and programmes that control him, and a deviant of the mechanic life. In the end, the 'lost' man for whom the robot is searching is the real hero, not the robot.

"My real dream is that poetry becomes, once again, a basic daily meal for the readers on the condition that the poet totally eliminates the inner distance within him and writes simply and, thus, the distance between him and the readers will vanish".

Is it immigration, or perhaps isolation, that created this work? Al-Shafiey, who has made his home in Saudi Arabia, continues: "It is important to bear in mind that immigration is not the physical absence from one's home country, but rather man's loss of his humanity, even though he is in his own country. It pleases me a lot to conclude with that stanza from 'Laughing Gases', the second part of The Complete Collection of a Robot:
The stranger who crosses the road
Does not need a white stick,
Nor a trained dog;
He needs the roads to have welcoming and tender eyes".

About the Author

Sharif Al-Shafiey was born in 1972 at Menouf in Lower Egypt. He received his B.A. in journalism from Cairo University, 1994. He is currently a journalist on the staff of *Al-Ahram Newspaper*. He is the author of five books, including *The Complete Collection of a Robot* (2012). His work has been translated from Arabic into English, French, Italian, and Spanish. "My Warm Clothes" appears here for the first time, translated by Amr El-Zawawy.

www.ingramcontent.com/pod-product-compliance
Lightning Source LLC
Chambersburg PA
CBHW051416090426
42737CB00014B/2701